LONDON WALKABOUT
WITH KATIE LUCAS
(The Top Ten Tourist Attractions)

Katie Lucas, who runs her own London based travel guiding
company, had travelled extensively herself. She has some 20
years' experience of the travel and guiding industry.

LONDON WALKABOUT WITH KATIE LUCAS

(The Top Ten Tourist Attractions)

Katie Lucas

SETTLE & BENDALL (WIGMORE)

First published in 1983 by
Settle & Bendall (Wigmore)
32 Savile Row
London W1X 1AG

Cover design by Jean Bird

ISBN 0 907070 19 1 (Hardback)
     0 907070 14 0 (Paperback)

All the maps in this book are reproduced by permission of Geographers' A-Z Map Co. Ltd. The maps are based upon the Ordnance Survey Map with the permission of the Controller of Her Majesty's Stationery Office, Crown Copyright Reserved.

The photographs in chapters 1, 2, 4 and 10 are reproduced by permission of The British Tourist Authority. Those in chapters 3 and 8 are by Joe Coté, in chapters 6 and 9 by Katie Lucas, and in chapter 7 by Mark Gwyn-Smith.

Printed in Great Britain by Villiers Publications Ltd,
26a Shepherds Hill, London N6 5AH

Contents

Preface

Many people come to London with definite ideas about the places they wish to see while they are here. After they have seen them they often have a feeling of anti-climax — they don't know where else to go. With this book in their hands there will be no turning backwards and forwards to find places to eat or walk. They will be taken at a gentle pace, on easy and attractive routes, which will show them not only the familiar landmarks, but also the hidden and often more interesting places. It will point out things they might otherwise miss. On the way it tells the relevant history, with fascinating anecdotes, which enliven the wealth of historical and architectural information it contains. It also tells them about some friendly pubs and restaurants at which to stop, as well as the necessary opening and closing times of the places to visit.

Introduction to London Walkabout

Walking is the best way of seeing all the sights of the city, because so much is hidden and difficult to see from cars and buses. One of the many delights of London is its courtyards and alleys and on foot one notices these and can make detours into them. The architectural features of houses and shops are more obvious, one can look over railings and peep into basements, one can see, at close quarters, all the details which give this 'town' its own particular personality. But first a few hints to help you on your way.

Taxis. When exhaustion point is reached London taxis are spacious, safe, and cheap. Their drivers are friendly and full of useful information — but don't forget that on top of the fare it is customary to add a tip of about 10%.

Buses. Normally buses are quite crowded but from the top deck of a double-decker you'll enjoy a wonderful bird's-eye view, well worth the perilous ascent up the stairs. A guide to London buses, and the Underground, as well as many other publications, can be obtained from the London Transport Information Bureau at 55, Broadway, SW1, which is between Queen Anne's Gate and Westminster Abbey and across the street from one of the pubs I recommend on the first walkabout.

The Underground (or Tube). The Underground system is extensive. There are nine lines and they all interconnect, so with the assistance of the Underground map, which is very clear and easy to read, you should have no problems. A free copy is available from ticket sellers at stations, or you can pick one up at the L.T.B. Information Bureau. In the booking halls of the Underground station, there are usually several machines selling tickets. Try to have correct change and look for an indicator board that tells the cost from the station you're in to the one you're headed for and check how much your fare will be. Then look for a machine displaying that amount, drop in your coins, and out will pop a yellow ticket. With the yellow ticket in hand, go to one of the barrier gates and put the ticket in the slot

9

indicated with the yellow side up. It will pop out of the top of the barrier as the doors open to let you through.

If you have no change, or all the foregoing is too much for you, go to the wooden cabin in the hall with the attendant inside selling green tickets. Just hand your money over and tell him where you want to go. The disadvantage of this method is that you may have to join a long queue, particularly in the rush hour. With a green ticket in your hand, you must go past the ticket collector, as it won't work the mechanical barrier.

With the aid of a map and a bit of intelligence, it is quite difficult to get lost in the Underground. Just don't let the sound of an approaching train stampede you at the last moment into rushing on to it unless you know for sure it's the right one. It will be no saving in time to go in the wrong direction, so take it slowly and you should have no difficulty.

Public Buildings. Remember that on entering any public building all bags and holdalls are searched. By keeping them tidy people in the queue behind won't see your choice collection of used paper handkerchiefs!

Hall Porters. Hall Porters can supply information on restaurants, air schedules, and just about everything else you need to know to make your stay easy and pleasant. They can also work miracles such as getting tickets for plays that have been booked up for months. They are Very Important People and run a mini-empire from their little corner of the hotel lobby. Treating them accordingly helps.

Drinking and Eating Simply While Day Tripping. Pubs are the great British Institution. There is nothing quite like them anywhere in the world. There are pubs to suit every taste. Some pubs sell bar snacks which can be very good, but most are probably cooked in a microwave oven — not very tasty, but nearly always good value for money. Some have proper restaurants, more expensive, but probably rather good English food, the most famous of these being the Cheshire Cheese which is in a little alley off Fleet Street. No hostelries survived the Great Fire of London in 1666, so in 1667 one of the first buildings to be put up was this little pub — the builders had to be refreshed as they went about their business of rebuilding London. It is a noisy, jolly, but inexpensive place, with restaurants on every floor. If the Maitre D'Hotel puts you on the ground floor you will see the settle that the great lexicographer, Dr. Samuel Johnson, used to sit on in the evenings when he held court in his corner by the fire. His house is just down the alley, and you'll see it on your third day's walk — down Fleet Street and the Strand. It isn't possible to book so turn up as early as possible after midday to be sure of getting seats, and you must be prepared to share a table.

Do remember that it is extremely difficult to find anything to eat outside the hours of 12-2 p.m. and 7-11 p.m. apart from a curry or a chop suey. If you are at all hungry, don't keep putting off the decision about the type of food you want or the restaurant at which you want to eat. Plunge now. Ten minutes may be too late! In London you will find almost every type of cuisine. In fact, the hardest thing to find is traditional English food. But for more information on restaurants consult the Good Food Guide or Egon Ronay.

Medical Help. If, after all this good eating, you wake up in the night with galloping indigestion, and you have no pills or medicines, help is at hand in Kilburn, where the 24 hour branch of Bliss the Chemist will supply anything you need to calm and soothe. Their address is 50, Willesden Lane, N.W.6. Their telephone number is 624 8000. If on the other hand you need a doctor during your stay, ask your Hall Porter.

Post Office. There is a 24 hour post office on the north-east side of Trafalgar Square.

Shopping. Most people who come to London have some idea of the shops they want to visit — Harrod's for almost everything, a must; Goode's for china, certainly; and probably Fortnum and Mason's for fine foodstuffs, especially since Jackson's of Piccadilly is no more. But added to these, everyone will have their own specialised shops they will want to spend time in, and there are so many selling so much delectable merchandise that it can be very tempting to neglect sight-seeing altogether and just shop. But just remember that every city in the world has shops with good buys, but not every city has the Changing of the Guard, so perhaps the ideal way of striking a good balance is to take one day off in every three for shopping and to pick a different area each time. But don't neglect the street markets, which can be great fun.

Special Anniversaries and Events. Finally, because London is such an historic city there are many ceremonies and events

11

taking place throughout the year. These are colourful and interesting, and if you are in the right place on the right day, well worth making a detour for. Not everyone can be in London for a Jubilee, but many people are in London for minor ceremonies of which they are completely unaware through lack of information. For example, on the 30th January the statue of Charles I at the south side of Trafalgar Square is decorated to commemorate the day he was beheaded in 1649. Afterwards there is a commemoration service at that gem of a church, St. Mary-le-Strand. On many other days throughout the year there are ceremonies like this going on in the capital, so for knowledge of them and for events in and around London visit the London Tourist Board at 4, Grosvenor Gardens, SW1. They also have a selection of local maps showing the location of theatres, cinemas, and other places of entertainment. For information about the many events that are on, not only in London but throughout the U.K., make a point early in your stay (I have included it in Chapter 2 — St. James's) to visit the British Tourist Authority in St. James's Street, where they have a wealth of information for the tourist.

Here is London. Enjoy it.

CHAPTER ONE

Opening and Closing Times
Trafalgar Square, Whitehall and Westminster

The National Gallery   Admission Daily 10.00-18.00
Trafalgar Square, W.C.2   Sundays 14.00-18.00
Not Dec 24/25, or Good Friday

Changing of the Horse Guards   11 a.m. Weekdays
Whitehall, S.W.1.   10 a.m. Sundays

Banqueting House   Tues.-Sat. 10.00-17.00
Whitehall, S.W.1.   Sundays 14.00-17.00

Jewel Tower   Weekdays 15th March –
Old Palace Yard, S.W.1   15th Oct. 9.30-18.30
16th October – 14th March 9.30-16.00

Abbey Garden   10.00 until dusk or 18.00
Great College Street, S.W.1   whichever is earlier

Lunch

Picnic in St. James's Park.
The Albert, Victoria St, S.W.1.
The Two Chairman, Tothill Street, S.W.1.

13

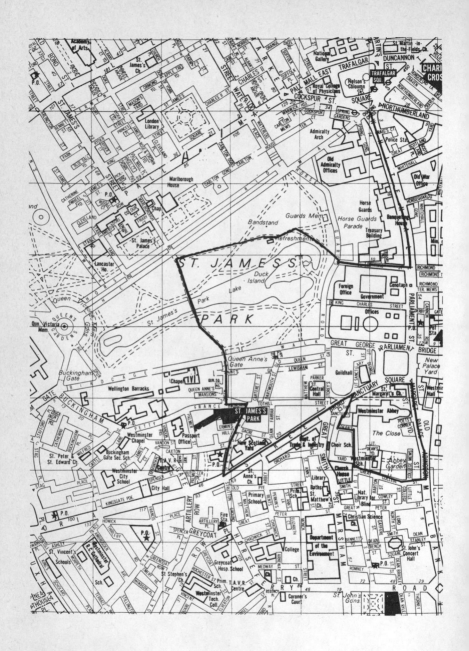

Trafalgar Square

Although Piccadilly is generally accepted as the heart of London, I find Trafalgar Square, dominated by Nelson on his column, more stirring, more truly alive, and far more beautiful. So I am using it as the starting point for these expeditions.

Before the 1820's the site of Trafalgar Square was a jumble of buildings and streets and stables. The Royal Mews, with the King's horses and coaches, had been here since 1300. But after the tragic death of Lord Nelson in 1805, on the deck of his flagship H.M.S. Victory, the nation's imagination was stirred. So, at the suggestion of the architect John Nash, an open space was cleared to create a piazza with which to commemorate the victory of Nelson at Trafalgar.

Trafalgar Square shows England at the height of her glory, with Nelson 167ft. 6½ins. up on his fluted Corinthian column, which was designed by Edmund Gosse in 1881, looking out in the direction of his heroic victory. He is guarded by four magnificent bronze lions, modelled by Landseer in 1867, and on the base of the column are reliefs made from captured French guns depicting Nelson's victories at St. Vincent, The Nile, Copenhagen, and of course, Trafalgar. The north of the square is raised to resemble the poop-deck of a man-of-war, with an outer rail of stone bollards. From here there is a wonderful view down Whitehall to Big Ben, which dominates the skyline at Westminster.

Behind this poop-deck, along the whole north side of the square, is the National Gallery, which was designed by William Wilkins in 1832 to house our national art collection. On the east side of the square is the imposing frontage of St. Martin-in-the-Fields, the masterpiece of James Gibbs, which he built in 1722. This is the parish church to Buckingham Palace, and to show its special status to the world, it has a gold crown at the top of its spire. It was in the previous church on this site that Charles II was christened, and the orange seller, Nell Gwynn, who became the best known of his many mistresses, was buried here.

16

There are several large buildings round the square, the most notable architecturally being Canada House, on the west, designed by Sir Robert Smirke in 1824, and on the east, South Africa House, designed by Sir Herbert Baker in 1935.

Diagonally across the south-west is Admiralty Arch, a triumphal arch, built by Sir Aston Webb in 1911, as part of the memorial to Queen Victoria. This leads into the Mall, the red-surfaced road leading to Buckingham Palace. Running parallel to the Mall is Pall Mall. It received this extraordinary name because Charles II introduced a game to England, after his exile in France, called Pell Mell, which was similar to croquet, and this is where it was played by the king and his courtiers.

In all weathers the square is a favourite meeting place for people and pigeons, but in the sun, the fountains, designed by Sir Edward Lutyens in 1948, sparkle and spray water lightly over the pavements, and provide a dipping place for pigeons. At night the fountains create a more dramatic mood when they are floodlit. Every Christmas the people of Norway send the gift of a fir tree to show their gratitude for the hospitality extended to their Royal Family during the last world war. This is placed in the square, brilliantly lit, and carols are sung round it each evening. This is one of London's special Christmas features.

Whitehall and Westminster

I think the first day should start with the Changing of the Guard, but not, as you might expect at Buckingham Palace, because, I think, the Changing of the Horse Guards in Whitehall is even more interesting.

Starting with Nelson on his column behind you, walk down Whitehall towards Big Ben. In the centre of the road, on a very hard-to-reach traffic island, is a statue of Charles I on horseback. He was the only English king to be beheaded and he is facing the scene of his death, on a very cold January day, in 1649. The statue, the most famous to be executed by the French sculptor Hubert le Seuer, was cast while he was alive, but after his death Lord Protector Oliver Cromwell ordered it to be destroyed and it was allegedly melted down. Small pieces of it were sold as mementoes to Royalist supporters. Imagine their surprise, when, after the Restoration of the Monarchy, the statue reappeared intact! Beside this statue, and set into the pavement, is a bronze plaque. This is the centre of London, and the point from which all distances are measured.

Walking on, along the west side of the road, you will pass the Old Admiralty building, a Georgian building by Thomas Ripley, built in 1723. It has a small courtyard hidden from the street by a very attractive stone screen, and an arched entranceway, surmounted by rearing sea-horses. This was the first public work by Robert Adam, who later went on to become one of the most prolific and successful designer/architects of all time. It was in this building, in 1805, that Admiral Nelson's body lay in state before being buried, with due pomp, in St. Paul's Cathedral.

A few more steps and you come to your first destination, the Horse Guards. This is the headquarters of the Commander-in-Chief of the Home Forces. You must arrive in plenty of time to be sure of a good vantage point, but before you take up your position have a look around at the pleasant grey stone building, with its low clock tower and two stone guard boxes. It was built by William Kent in 1760 on the site of the old tiltyard of Whitehall Palace, and although you may no longer see knights galloping at each other on gaily caparisoned chargers, you can, if you look in the guards' boxes, see the Horseguards, in their gleaming breastplates and helmets, sitting on what could well be descendants of those very same chargers.

The Queen's Bodyguard is made up of two cavalry regiments, the Blues and Royals, and the Life Guards, and they take it in turn to do a twenty-four hour guard duty at Horse Guards. The mounted sentries being relieved every hour, and then dismounted every two hours.

At the rear of the courtyard are three arches, which lead to an open parade ground. This is called Horse Guards Parade, and this is where the Queen, on her official birthday on a Saturday at the beginning of June, reviews the Trooping of the Colour, a ceremony that includes all the Guards regiments, their bands, and her Majesty riding side-saddle in a long skirted uniform. This is a spectacular occasion, full of pageantry and colour. On this day the parade is closed to the general public, as only invited guests may sit in the stands which are built every year round the Parade ground, but a good view of the processions to and from Buckingham Palace can be found on either side of the Mall.

The Horse Guards are quartered in the Household Cavalry Barracks in Hyde Park at Knightsbridge. They leave the barracks at 10.30 and walk through the Park to Hyde Park Corner, down Constitution Hill to Buckingham Palace, down the Mall, and at three minutes to eleven you will see them turn the corner and approach Horse Guards Parade — taking up their places on the Parade ground as the clock strikes eleven — they are never late. When the Queen is in residence the troop of twelve men is swelled by the addition of the Queen's Trumpeter, an Officer and a Standard Bearer. While watching the ceremony remember the guardsmen you see here and elsewhere in London are not just toy soldiers. After their tour of ceremonial duty they will return to their khaki and flak jackets and become professional soldiers of the twentieth century British Army. Equally at home with tanks, mechanised carriers, recoilless weapons, as they are guarding Buckingham Palace or the Horse Guards.

After the ceremony, watch the old guard ride away. This is

one of the most evocative sights and sounds of London, with their plumed helmets, gleaming breastplates, and the clinking of the harness. Watch as they disappear down the Mall and you will catch glimpses of them through the trees in St. James's Park.

Now return to Whitehall and cross the street to the Banqueting House. This magnificent building was designed by Inigo Jones in 1619 and it is the only surviving building of the old Palace of Whitehall which was the home of the Kings of England from 1529 to 1698. Until 1529 it was the London palace of the Archbishops of York. Then it was seized by Henry VIII from Cardinal Wolsey. He was the Archbishop of the time, and he must have become very displeased with the King's grasping behaviour, especially when in 1529 he also lost his other sumptuous palace, Hampton Court, in the same way. The King extended the palace, turning it into his principal residence. He then brought his new wife Anne Boleyn there on their wedding day from the Tower of London. Subsequently their daughter, the young Princess Elizabeth, who later became Queen Elizabeth I, was taken from there to the Tower on the orders of her half-sister, Bloody Mary, when she became Queen in 1553. The King himself died there in 1547, but not before marrying another of his wives, Jane Seymour, in the palace in 1536.

The rest of the palace went up in flames in 1698, when in an attic, a laundress was drying clothes before a charcoal brazier. She started a fire she could not put out and perished in the flames. All that was left of the palace were a few walls and the Banqueting House.

The Banqueting House is a double cube room, being one hundred and ten feet long, fifty-five feet wide, and fifty-five feet high. The glory of it is the ceiling which was painted by Sir Peter Paul Rubens, for which he was given £3,000 and a knighthood. The paintings depict the apotheosis of James I, the first of the Stuart kings, whose son Charles I, stepped from one of these windows to his beheading on the block. Oliver Cromwell, the man responsible for his death, and who took over the reins of power, died in the palace, but from natural causes, nine years later in 1658.

As you walk along Whitehall, past a statue of Sir Walter Raleigh, with the huge bulk of the Ministry of Defence behind it, you will see the Cenotaph, the memorial to the dead of two world wars. It was designed by Sir Edward Lutyens in 1919 and it is the scene of a very moving ceremony on the Sunday nearest to November 11th every year, when the traffic comes to a halt, and the Queen, members of the Royal family, Prime Minister, Cabinet Ministers, etc., and the thousands of ordinary men and women who want to pay homage, gather round the Cenotaph. At 10.59 the Queen lays a wreath at the foot of the Cenotaph and one minute later a gun is fired to mark the beginning of two minutes of silent prayer, which is ended by the firing of a second gun.

Most of the buildings facing the Cenotaph are government offices, but on the same side of the road as Horse Guards is an unpretentious little street which has two policemen at the entrance monitoring the vehicles as they come and go. This is Downing Street, and No. 10 is the official residence of the Prime Minister. Sometimes, for reasons of security, the street is blocked off to pedestrians, but when it is open there is always a small crowd standing on the pavement opposite No. 10, waiting hopefully to see some important personage.

By walking straight along Downing Street, past No.10 and down the steps at the end, you will come to one of the prettiest parks in London — St. James's Park. This was the deer park to Henry VIII, as it lay conveniently between Whitehall Palace and his newly built palace of St. James's. During the reign of Charles II the public were allowed entry to see the King feeding the birds in the Royal Aviary surrounded by his Court, and it has been open to the public ever since.

If the weather is good it is very pleasant to have lunch in the park. Buy a snack and some coffee at the kiosk, or be prepared and take a picnic. A military band plays in the bandstand between one and two during the summer months, so sit in a deckchair, with your food, and listen to the band. A deckchair attendant will come and collect a few pence. St. James's Park is a bird sanctuary. Very fat and tame birds they are, too, because they are given the crusts and crumbs of the people who take their lunches to the park.

After this pleasant interlude a gentle stroll through the park will bring you to your next destination. Walk over the bridge and pause to enjoy the view of the roofs of Whitehall, probably

21

one of the more photographed sights in London. If you are lucky you may see the pelicans who brave the climate and live on an island in the lake.

Once over the bridge follow the middle path to Birdcage Walk, a lovely name which commemorates the Aviary that James I had here. Across the road you will see a gate in the black railings which is Queen Anne's Gate. Built in 1704 by William Paterson it is named afterEngland's fattest queen, who was the youngest daughter of James II. The street of attractive red brick houses you will see when you are through the gate was also built by Paterson, and with their elaborate canopied entrances they are among the most complete examples of Queen Anne domestic architecture in London.

While you are in the area it is worth a slight detour to 55, The Broadway, the headquarters of London Transport, for information and booklets. If you have not already lunched in the park there are two pubs in this area which are good places to lunch. The first is the Two Chairmen in Tothill Street, a fascinating two-hundred-year-old pub, small and smoky, with an enormous lunch-time trade from the local offices and from New Scotland Yard which is just around the corner. They only sell bar snacks, i.e. sausages and mash, and if you require something more substantial there is an equally pleasant but larger pub close by – The Albert in Victoria Street, which has bar snacks on the ground floor, but on the first floor there is a pleasant carvery.

After lunch look for the twin towers of the great west porch of Westminster Abbey and walk towards them. The Abbey is the most important ecclesiastical monument in England. Most English monarchs have been crowned, and many married and buried here. The church as we see it today was built in 1245 by Henry III to honour the last of the Anglo-Saxon kings, the very saintly Edward the Confessor, who built the previous church on this site. His body was taken from its resting place in that church and was placed in the very elaborate tomb in the most holy part of the Abbey, the Chapel of St. Edward the Confessor. As you enter you will be struck by the loftiness of the interior, the tallest in a Gothic church in England. The pillars of Purbeck marble support a double triforium and above that is a clerestory. Looking down the nave you will see the beautiful Waterford glass chandeliers given by the Guinness family in 1965 to commemorate the 900th anniversary of the Consecration of the church of Edward the Confessor.

Just inside the entrance there are several things of great interest, one of them being the earliest known painting of an English king, Richard II. It is believed that it was painted in 1380. Although he was deposed in 1399, and probably murdered in Pontefract Castle, he is buried in the Chapel of Edward the Confessor where he shares an elaborate tomb with his first wife, Anne of Bohemia.

On the floor is a large slab of black marble from Belgium covering the tomb of the unknown soldier – an English soldier, lying in French soil. Close to this is another marble slab, green this time, which is the memorial to Sir Winston Churchill. He is not buried here though, but in the family graveyard of the Dukes of Marlborough, whose cousin he was, at Bladon in Oxfordshire. Another interesting memorial just here is a stone which marks the spot where the body of the great Victorian philanthropist George Peabody lay, at the request of Queen Victoria, before being returned to his native Massachusetts in a Royal Navy vessel.

Everywhere you look in this magnificent church there are tablets and monuments, although not everybody who is commemorated here is buried here, and some, like Ben Jonson the playwright, have three different memorials to them!

After you walk through the heavily gilded choir screen, which like the choir fittings dates from the 1830's, you will find yourself in the Sanctuary. It is here beneath the lantern, and in front of the High Altar, that the Coronation Chair is placed when the Monarch is crowned by the Archbishop of Canterbury.

When you leave the Sanctuary you will pass the Chapels of Abbot Islip, which is not open, St. John the Baptist, which is and is certainly worth going into to see the extraordinarily elaborate tomb of Lord Hunsdon, and St. Paul, which also contains some fascinating tombs. Then you ascend a flight of steps which leads to a pair of magnificent bronze-covered oak doors, which depict the heraldic emblems of Henry VII because this is Henry VII's Chapel. On the north side of the aisle is the tomb of the two Tudor half-sisters, Elizabeth I and Mary I, daughters of Henry VIII. Although enemies in life they were buried in the same tomb, but only Elizabeth's effigy is displayed on it – and very hawk-like it is too. This tomb was erected to Elizabeth by James I of England who was also James VI of Scotland. He succeeded her on the throne, and therefore united the two ever-warring kingdoms.

The far end of the aisle is called 'Innocents' Corner'. In a beautiful casket designed by Sir Christopher Wren, are the remains of the two little Princes in the Tower, Edward V and his younger brother, Richard, Duke of York, the two young sons of Edward IV. Legend has it that Richard III, their uncle, had them murdered in the Tower of London in 1483 and took the crown from the elder. Edward was born in the Abbey when his mother was seeking sanctuary there.

In the south aisle are three magnificent tombs. The first is the Countess of Lennox, who was the mother of Lord Darnley, the second husband of Mary, Queen of Scots, and father of Mary's only child James I, and therefore grandmother to the first King of England and Scotland. Then there is the tomb of the beautiful Mary herself, and do take note of the Lion Rampant at her feet. After her beheading in Fotheringay Castle her remains were placed in Peterborough Cathedral, but after her son came to the throne he ordered them to be brought to the Abbey and built this fine tomb to house them. The last tomb in the north aisle is of the saintly Margaret Beaufort, who was the mother of Henry VII who built this chapel.

Henry VII's Chapel is probably the most beautiful part of the Abbey. The vaulted ceiling is superb, and over the tomb of Henry VII and his queen, Elizabeth of York, there are gilded royal emblems, including the Tudor Rose. The Tudor Rose symbolises the peace that was restored to England after the Wars of the Roses, when the red rose of Lancashire, which represents Henry VII, married the white rose of York as represented by his wife the Yorkist heiress Elizabeth. In front of the tomb of the Founder is the grave of his grandson, Edward VI, the only son of Henry VIII. He was a sickly child, who came to the throne at ten and died at sixteen, leaving his half-sister, Mary I, to take the Throne of England.

On the other side of the Founder's tomb is the Battle of Britain Chapel. It has an interesting window which depicts the

Battle of Britain and which incorporates the badges of all the Fighter Squadrons which took part. The Abbey was heavily sandbagged during World War II, but under the window you will see a hole in the stonework. This was made by a fragment of a German bomb during the Battle of Britain in September 1940 so it was appropriately left.

At the front of the chapel look down, and on a small slab at your feet you will see an inscription which tells you that Oliver Cromwell was buried here. He died of natural causes and was buried with due ceremony in the Abbey. When the monarchy was restored three years later his body was dug up, and beheaded, and his head displayed on Westminster Hall! Henry VII's Chapel is the chapel of the Order of the Bath, an order of chivalry of which the Prince of Wales is the Great Master. The Helms and Colours of the Knights are on the stalls.

You will now walk over a bridge past the tomb of Henry V of Agincourt fame, and through a screen which is his Chantry Chapel; you are now in the Confessor's Chapel. In the centre is the Shrine of Saint Edward, with recesses in which the sick would huddle through the night in the hope of being cured. Probably the most notable tomb, apart from the Confessor's, is the plainest. It is the tomb of Edward I and it is enormous. He was 6ft. 2in. tall, and as he died in 1307 when most people didn't top 5ft. 2in. you can see why he was called Edward Longshanks! He was also called the Hammer of the Scots, and in one of his forays into Scotland in 1297 he stole the Stone of Scone, the traditional coronation stone of the Scots. This is now incorporated into the Coronation Chair and therefore symbolises the union between the two countries. As you will see by the size of the stone it must make it very heavy to move the Coronation Chair to its position in the Sanctuary when it is used at Coronations. Edward I was also the first king to be crowned in the Abbey.

After you leave the Confessor's Chapel, and as you walk to Poet's Corner you pass more side chapels, St. Nicholas, SS Edmund and Thomas the Martyr which both have some very fine tombs, and the Chapel of St. Benedict which is not open. Poet's Corner is one of the most interesting parts of the Abbey, with memorials to many authors, poets, and musicians. There are so many well-known names it's like meeting old friends, but the original poet in this corner was Geoffrey Chaucer who died in 1400 and whose tiny tomb you can see on the east wall. In fact, as he died exactly one hundred years after Edward I, it's interesting to compare the difference in size!

Now visit the Cloisters where there is a brass rubbing centre. On your left you will come to the Chapter House which was built in 1245. It is an octagonal room which is 56ft in diameter with one single column to the roof. It is beautiful, and very light, and historically very important, because this is where the early House of Commons met from 1257 until 1547, when it moved across the road to St. Stephen's Chapel in the Palace of Westminster.

The third doorway on your left, which is notable because of seven huge locks, is the Chamber of the Pyx. This was a chapel in the previous church on this site. But it was subsequently used to house the sacred relics and treasures of the Abbey and also the Pyx, the standard against which gold and silver currency was measured, tested and weighed.

Finally walk round the Cloisters and under the archway. Turn left and as you walk towards another archway at the end of the pavement, look into the courtyards on your left, because you are passing Westminster School, one of the great public schools of England, founded by Elizabeth I in 1560.

Through the archway turn left. You are now walking beside a high ragstone wall, built in 1374, which encloses one of the oldest gardens in England, perhaps a thousand years old, where the monks grew herbs for medicinal purposes. This garden is open to the public on Thursdays.

On the other side of the road are streets of attractive Georgian houses. As you will see the houses are very close to Parliament. A vote in Parliament is called a Division, and eight minutes before the vote, the Division Bell rings to warn the Members to come to vote. Members of Parliament lucky enough and rich enough to afford houses in this area can have a division bell installed in their house, giving them eight minutes to reach the House of Commons to vote, so this is known as the Division Bell area.

Walk across the little green, past the sculpture called 'Knife Edge' by Henry Moore, and you will see a small stone tower which is dwarfed by Westminster Abbey. This is Edward III's

Jewel Tower, a gem in itself, standing beside the remains of a water-lily planted moat. It was built in 1366 to hold the Royal plate and jewellery for the Palace of Westminster. It is very small but well worth visiting.

As you leave the Jewel Tower and walk past the statue of George V by Sir W. Reid Dick and Sir Giles Scott, you will see a church beside Westminster Abbey. This is St. Margaret's, Westminster, which is the parish church to the House of Commons. Since it was built in 1500 it has been the scene of many fashionable weddings. Among the famous people who have married here are Samuel Pepys, the great diarist, and Sir Winston and Lady Churchill. The east window has a fascinating history because it was made in 1501 to celebrate the bethrothal of Henry VIII's elder brother Prince Arthur to Catherine of Aragon. Sadly Prince Arthur died, and as we all know Henry married Catherine. The window found a resting place here in 1758. Another interesting window is over the West door and it is dedicated by Americans to the memory of Sir Walter Raleigh, who was beheaded across the road in Old Palace Yard at the Palace of Westminster, and whose body lies in front of the altar. One of the great Englishmen!

CHAPTER TWO

Opening and Closing Times
St. James's

Marlborough House   Sat., Sun., Bank Hols. 14.00-18.00
             Easter-September

Lancaster House   Sat., Sun., Bank Hols 14.00-18.00
            Easter-November 30th

The Changing of the Guard Daily 11.30. until 1st Sept,
     when every 2nd day until 1st April

Burlington House   Daily 10.00-18.00,
    except Christmas Day, Boxing Day

Breakfast
Bonbonniere Cafe, Duke Street, S.W.1.

Lunch
The Red Lion, Crown Passage, S.W.1.
The Blue Posts, Bennet Street, S.W.1.
The Guinea, Bruton Place, W.1.

Tea
The Soda Fountain, Fortnum and Mason, Piccadilly.

St. James's

For the second of what I hope is going to be a series of memorable holiday walks in one of the world's most exciting cities. you could start with a really good breakfast. St James's is one of the many small villages of which London is made up, albeit one of the grandest. It is very close to Buckingham Palace, but from the time Whitehall Palace burnt down to the time Buckingham Palace superseded it, St. James's Palace was the principal London residence of the sovereign. As a result, from the early 18th. century onwards, many very fine houses were built there, and it later became renowned for its bachelor apartments for 'young men about town', some real like Beau Brummel, some literary like Raffles.

The most exclusive and renowned of Gentlemen's Clubs are in this area. Discreet, but obvious because of the magnificence of their frontages. The Gentlemen's gentlemen would have had their own meeting places to gather and discuss the business of their masters' exploits. Such a place is the Bonbonniere Cafe in Duke Street where I suggest you go for breakfast.

This little cafe is the haunt of people from the world famous auction rooms, Christies, journalists from The Economist, the weekly journal about the economic scene, and many other varied day-time and night-time inhabitants of St. James's, including debutantes and their beaux. It is very friendly and bustling. From there you can walk to Clarence House, the London home of the Queen Mother, where at 9 a.m., on her birthday August 4th, you can hear a piper playing his bagpipes for the Scottish-born Queen Mother.

Walk down to the end of Duke Street, cross over and walk through the little passage in front of you called Crown Passage (incidentally, the Red Lion pub you will see there is a good lunching place). At the end you will see St. James's Palace.

It is very picturesque, a mini Tudor palace with a lovely gate-house on Pall Mall which has a sentry on duty. It was built by

31

Good King Hal — or bad King Henry, depending on how you feel about that rogue Tudor, King Henry VIII. His need for yet another palace cannot have been very great because in London alone he owned the Palace of Westminster (which unfortunately was badly damaged by fire in 1512), The Palace of Whitehall, The Tower of London (although he only seemed to use that for marrying and beheading his wives — he did both activities there twice!), Hampton Court Palace, Sheen Palace, and the Palace of Placentia at Greenwich.

He bought the land in 1531 and built his palace, to which he brought Anne Boleyn, their initials are carved over one of the doors. Although no longer the residence of the Sovereign, the British Court is still officially the Court of St. James's and when a new sovereign is proclaimed it is here, from the balcony in Friary Court, 'The King is dead, Long Live the King'.

It cannot be visited because the various apartments are occupied by members of the Royal Household, but this makes it exciting, because, as you walk past the black painted doors you notice shiny brass plates on which are names like The Lord Chamberlain. While you are there do notice the street lamps, they really are lovely, black iron surmounted by gold crowns. Although the Palace cannot be visited both the Chapel Royal and the Queen's Chapel can, and you can go to services in both. The Chapel Royal is in the Palace, and although much changed in the 19th. century it still has a very fine ceiling, reputedly designed by Holbein. The Queen's Chapel is across the road. It was designed by Inigo Jones, who designed the Banqueting House. Like the Chapel Royal its great beauty is the ceiling, and like the Banqueting House it is a double cube. It was built in 1623. It was from here that Charles I received the sacrament before walking across St. James's Park to the Banqueting House to be beheaded.

As the Changing of the Guard takes place at 11.30 a.m., a stroll along Pall Mall to the Duke of York's Steps, and then along the Mall to Buckingham Palace would be enjoyable.

Walking eastwards you pass a great many clubs. First you pass the Oxford and Cambridge, then the R.A.C., the Army and Navy, the Junior Carlton, the Travellers, the Reform, and the Atheneum. Most of the Gentlemen's clubs of London developed from the 17th. c. coffee and chocolate houses, where men of similar interests could meet and exchange news and information. Many of the clubs were gaming clubs, such as Arthur's Club, which is now the Carlton — one of the most elite!

On the opposite side of the road from the Palace, not far from Crown Passage, is a clockmakers called Dents. They made the clock which is world famous — and mistakenly called Big Ben — in fact the bell with the distinctive chime is Big Ben.

When you reach Waterloo Place — named of course after the Duke of Wellington's most famous victory, and whose mounting block still stands in the Square — look south towards the Steps, and you will see a granite column 124ft. high. It is the Duke of York's Column. The Duke of York was the second son of George III, and was Commander-in-Chief of the British Army. He was supposedly very profligate, living too well, spending too much, but a very good administrator and very popular with his soldiers. When he died every officer and man in the Army contributed a day's pay to put him on the column out of the reach of his creditors! Up there he has a wonderful view of the tree tops in St. James's Park, the Horse Guards, and Westminster, but standing on the steps beneath him so do we. On a level with us as we stand admiring the view is Carlton House Terrace, a superb terrace of houses, once the homes of the aristocracy, and designed by John Nash who also redesigned Buckingham Palace for George IV in 1825.

Among the people who have lived here were Lord Curzon, Viceroy of India, to whom a statue is erected outside his house, and in No. 4 Carlton Gardens, General de Gaulle had his Free French Headquarters in World War II.

After you descend the Steps turn right and walk along the sandy path towards Buckingham Palace. It is a very pleasant walk under the plane trees.

You pass the gardens of Marlborough House which is an enormous mansion built by Sir Christopher Wren in 1709 for the Duke of Marlborough, the victor of Blenheim. It has been lived in by many members of the Royal Family including, when they were Princes of Wales, Edward VII and George V. When not being used for commonwealth occasions, its principal use now, it is open to the public.

Continue walking, and after St. James's Palace the next building you will see is Clarence House, the home of the Queen Mother. Built by John Nash in 1825 for William IV, it is of course a private house so not open to the public.

The last house in this row of marvellous houses is Lancaster House, designed and built by Wyatt in 1825 for the Duke of York — and when you see the magnificence of Lancaster House you can see why he ended up on the column! It is used as a Government hospitality centre, but, like Marlborough House, may be visited at weekends between Easter and Christmas, when it is not in use for Government entertaining, and a very worthwhile visit it will be. It's most striking feature is the double marble-lined staircase, but the furniture, fittings, and pictures, are all exceptionally fine. It was in this house that Chopin played to Queen Victoria.

Now you come to an open circus in front of Buckingham Palace. It is very attractive with a stone balustrade, wrought iron screens, colourful flowers, and beautifully mown lawns. In the centre is the memorial to Queen Victoria. It was designed by Sir Aston Webb in 1911 and sculpted by Sir Thomas Brock. The allegorical groups represent the virtues and achievements of Victorian England. As the time for the Changing of the Guard gets closer, more and more people will cram onto the memorial, because it does give almost the best vantage point for viewing behind the Palace railings, unless you are lucky enough, and early enough, to get there in time to be in the front row on the railings. If the Queen is in residence the Royal Standard will be flying above the Palace.

There are five Guards Regiments. The Grenadier, the Scots, the Welsh, the Irish, and the Coldstream. The Coldstream claim they are the senior regiment, and the Grenadier that they are, so they form up first or last, and the motto of the Coldstream Guards is 'Nulli Secundus' — second to none! All these regiments take it in turn to guard Buckingham Palace.

The ceremony takes place at 11.30 a.m. but as they march to and from their barracks, they are accompanied by a band — and depending on which regiment is taking over, often by a mascot. Like the Pied Piper the band always has a crowd of people following it, scurrying along the pavement beside it, caught up in the magic of the bagpipes, pipes and drums, or brass.

34

Whichever it is, it is always a stirring sight, and it is fascinating that men who are blowing so hard can march so fast!

After the ceremony the old guard marches off to its barracks and as people walk away, you will have an opportunity to look at Buckingham Palace. It was built for the Duke of Buckingham, who was a distinguished politician in the reigns of both Charles II and James II, but he ended his days in disgrace, because under the reign of Queen Anne, whose suitor he had been in his youth, he plotted for the return of the Stuarts. He was possibly influenced in this by the woman he *did* marry, Catherine, who was the illegitimate daughter of Catherine Sedley and James II, therefore with a great deal of Stuart blood in her veins. Buckingham Palace was purchased by George III in 1762 for his Queen. It was then a country house outside the gates of London. Not much seems to have happened to it until 1825 when it was remodelled for George IV by John Nash. Nash turned it from a fairly ordinary country house, into a palace, although at the time that was not the intention, because it wasn't until the accession of Queen Victoria to the throne in 1837 that it became the official residence of the sovereign. The facade you now see is of this century. It was designed in 1913 by Sir Aston Webb, who designed the Victoria Memorial and Admiralty Arch. So we can thank him for the magnificence of the view from Trafalgar Square, through Admiralty Arch, and down the Mall to the Palace.

At this point you could either take a pleasant and leafy stroll through the 53 acres of Green Park or an equally pleasant one up St. James's Street. Green Park is another of London's Royal Parks. Created in 1668 by Charles II, a man who liked to enjoy himself, it was the scene of many Royal picnics. To make these occasions even more enjoyable it had an ice house to cool the wine and drinks on hot summer days. On the east side is a paved walk called Queen's Walk which gives a very good view of the houses which are built overlooking the path. The association with Charles II continues with the site on which the present Bridgewater House stands, itself an interesting house built by Barry in 1841. The previous house on the site was presented by Charles to Barbara Villiers, Duchess of Cleveland, another of his many mistresses. Apparently he liked to be able to talk to them over the garden wall! Lord Beaverbrook, the Canadian born press lord, lived in Stornaway House and then as he became older, moved into an apartment in Arlington House, a little further up the Walk. The final, and very grand building at the corner of the Walk and Piccadilly, is the Ritz Hotel. Built in 1904, and one of the 'Ritziest' of London's many hotels.

If you choose the other walk through St. James's Street, it is like going back in time. Many of the shop fronts are original. Walk slowly up the street looking at Lock and Co., the hatters, Lobbs, the bootmakers, and Berry Bros. and Rudd, wine merchants, who have been in the same shop since 1723!

On the right is King Street, which leads into St. James's Square. One of the oldest squares in London, it was also the first to be built after the Great Fire of London. The oldest surviving house in the Square is No. 4. It was built in 1676. It was in this Square that Nancy, Lady Astor lived, the first woman Member of Parliament and the first American to become an M.P. When the Square was first laid out by the Earl of St. Albans in the 1660's there was a boating lake in the middle.

Back in St. James's Street you will find, half way up, the British Tourist Authority. It is worth a few minutes to go in and find out what is going on in town. They also have information on many events that happen in Britain.

If you have spent too long ambling up St. James's, maybe taking a detour into the courtyards that line it on right and left, you might be feeling hungry. The turning on the left after the B.T.A. is Bennet Street, and a few yards along is a pub called the Blue Posts. This is a popular lunching place — justly renowned for its prime rib of roast beef, and if that sounds too large a lunch to face when you have an afternoon's walking ahead of you, the downstairs Blue Posts Bar serves hot and cold snacks. If, however, you still feel you have some walking time ahead of you before lunch, walk on to Piccadilly. If it is a weekend don't cross the road, stroll along the side of Green Park looking at the pictures which hang there on Saturdays and Sundays, and which are for sale. Then, when you can, cross the road. The traffic is fast and bad-tempered here, so be careful.

Walk down Berkeley Street. Here you will see the car showrooms of the most elegant cars — Rolls-Royce, Bentley, Jaguar. This street leads into Berkeley Square where there are seats to sit down. You are now in Mayfair, an expensive and fashionable area. Annabel's, the most select of nightclubs, occupies one of the most elegant houses in the Square. John Priestley, the discoverer of oxygen, lived in the Square until 1794 when he emigrated to Pennsylvania. Just out of the top of the Square to the left is the Connaught, one of the very best of English hotels. But if you go to the right at the top of the Square you will see Bruton Place. Down there is a pub called The Guinea. Again, marvellous roasts, but rather expensive. Instead perhaps, a very pleasant thing to do on a warm day when the street outside is full of people drinking beer and eating sausage rolls and pies, is to join them.

Walk back into Berkeley Square and turn left and left again, now you are in Bruton Street. A small street full of very fine shops. At No. 17, when it was still a private house, the Queen was born. First comes Culpeper House, a wonderland of herbs and spices, used medicinally or to enrich bath-time and your skin.

There are fur showrooms and Art Galleries, but for the really covetable goodies Algernon Asprey is the shop — not all wildly expensive but all beautiful. On the corner of Bruton Street and Bond Street is the Ireland House Shop. There you will find warm and chunky Aran sweaters. Still really knitted by the wives of fishermen, but now not only for fishermen.

Bond Street was laid out in 1686 by Sir Thomas Bond, and is now one of London's most select shopping streets. So turn right towards Piccadilly. There are so many marvellous shops to look at here that you will need no guidelines from me. If you collect Meerschaum pipes, amber, glass, china, jewellery, antiques, pictures, they are all to be found. Also Sotheby's the fine art auctioneers, as well as clothes shops, and hairdressers. One of the most famous people who has lived in Bond Street was Admiral Lord Nelson, he of the column, at No. 147.

When you reach Burlington Gardens turn left, Savile Row is in front of you, the street world renowned for men's tailoring. To the right is Burlington Arcade. This attractive and fascinating row of little shops, ranged each side of a covered arcade, was built in 1819 by Lord George Cavendish, who lived in Burlington House next door. He built it 'For the gratification of the publick and to give employment to industrious females'. Although it suffered bombing in the second world war it is now as good as new. The intimate friendly atmosphere is unique, and although a little on the pricey side, people from all over the world come here to shop. It is open 9 to 5.30, and 9 to 1 p.m. on Saturdays. At each end of the Arcade there are beadles. A sinecure for ex-N.C.O.'s of the 10th Hussars, which was the regiment of Lord Chesham who owned the Arcade from 1879 to 1926.

Try to time your exit on to Piccadilly for the hour — because on the hour Mr. Fortnum and Mr. Mason, who founded that wonderful store, come out of their rooms in the clock which is facing you on the front of the store, one carrying a tray, and the other carrying a candelabra, and a very bell-like rendering of the Eton Boating Song is played.

Piccadilly is believed to be named after a tailor who built a house in the area in 1611. He specialised in making a type of ruff called a 'Piccadilly'. With the fortune he made from these he built the house, and people nicknamed it Piccadilly Hall. When the street was extended in 1627 the name stuck.

To the left is Burlington House, one of the few detached mansions remaining in the Mayfair area. It has been much altered — having been owned by many people since it was built by the 1st Earl of Burlington in 1664. Each new owner liked to change things to suit their taste, and if they were rich enough to own Burlington House they were rich enough to employ the best architects and designers to carry out radical changes. The Government purchased it in 1853 for £140,000 to house the Royal Academy, and new buildings were added in 1869 by R. R. Banks and Charles Barry for the use of various learned societies, such as the British Academy, the Royal Astronomical Society, the Chemical Society, the Society of Antiquaries, the Linnean Society, and the Geological Society. Officially the opening event of the London 'season' is the Private View at the Royal Academy, it is very fashionable and by invitation only. After Private View day it is open to anyone and is well worth visiting. In the winter, interesting special exhibitions are held here.

The next entrance down Piccadilly is Albany. It is very discreet and very hidden. It was designed for Lord Melbourne in 1771, by Sir William Chambers, and was acquired by Frederick, Duke of York and Albany in 1791. In 1802 it was divided into fashionable sets of rooms — or chambers. It is an

38

extremely private place, and among the occupants in recent times have been Edward Heath and Terence Stamp, the film actor. Among the past occupants have been the Literary Lords, Byron, Macauley, and Lytton.

After all that walking you now deserve the treat of afternoon tea at the Soda Fountain in Fortnum and Mason. So cross Piccadilly to the south side, and enjoy the atmosphere and the smells of that most marvellous of emporiums. Even in the grocery department the assistants wear frock coats!

CHAPTER THREE

Opening and Closing Times
The Strand

Prince Henry's Room   13.45-17.00, not Sundays
17, Fleet St., E.C.4   Saturday 13.45-16.30

Middle Temple Hall   10.00-12.00, 15.00-16.45, not Sundays
Middle Temple, E.C.4

Dr. Johnson's House   11.00-17.00, not Sundays
17, Gough Square, E.C.4

The Royal Courts of Justice   8.00-dusk, not Sundays.
The Strand, W.C.2

Lunch
Simpsons Old English Restaurant, 100 Strand, W.C.2
The Cheshire Cheese, Wine Office Court, Fleet Street, London
E.C.4.

Tea
The Royal Courts of Justice Cafe

The Strand

The Strand is the noisiest street in London — it's true, the decibel counter says so. It starts at Charing Cross Station, where in the station yard is a replica of the last Eleanor Cross. Edward I adored his wife Eleanor of Castile, and when she died at Lincoln in 1290 he had her brought to London for burial at Westminster Abbey. They rested 13 nights on the journey, and at each place a cross was erected to commemorate this, the last one being here at Charing Cross. Although this is not the original stone cross, it is a replica of it.

After the station yard take the first alley on the right which is called Villiers Street. It is a lane with cheap shops and sandwich bars in it, and hurrying crowds because it runs between two very busy stations, Charing Cross at the top of the hill, which is the main line station for Kent, and Embankment at the bottom, an Underground station.

Just before Embankment, there is a gate on the left into Embankment Gardens. Walk through the gate and even on a miserable day the gardens are a pleasure to be in. They are beautifully tended, and there is a bandstand, so that when opportunity allows, a return trip to listen to the band would be a pleasant thing to do. There is a particularly fine view of the Festival Hall across the river from here, and on the other side of the Embankment you will see Cleopatra's Needle. It was erected here in 1878, although it dates from 1500 B.C. Its partner is in Central Park, New York.

At the back of the gardens is a very fine watergate. It was the watergate to York House, the home of the very rich and powerful Duke of Buckingham, the handsome favourite of King James I and King Charles I, but, confusingly, not the same Duke of Buckingham as the Buckingham House Duke.

Until the four Scottish brothers Adam started to build the Adelphi in 1768, the Thames was very much wider than it is today. The brothers built the first embankment, buying the site of Durham House, the London house of the Bishops of

43

Durham, and creating for the first time a riverside quay with vaults built on it, then the houses magnificently built on the vaults. Apart from the Watergate the Duke of Buckingham is still remembered by the street names. His full name was George Villiers, Duke of Buckingham. Every part of this name was used — even down to 'Of Alley', now, sadly, renamed York Place, still a name with a sense of history but not so eccentric.

From the Watergate walk up Buckingham Street, an attractive small street, with nice old houses, and with many associations. Samuel Pepys lived in two of the houses, 12 and 14, and in 1697 Peter the Great lived in a house on the site of what is now Burdett House.

Turn right into John Adam Street, and you can get an idea of how the Adelphi must once have looked. There are still some of the elegant Adam houses standing. Probably the grandest is No. 8 which houses the Royal Society of Arts. The Society was founded in 1754 to encourage the Arts, Manufacture, and Commerce. It moved into its present building in 1774.

After turning into Adam Street, and before returning to the bustle of the Strand, walk to the Adelphi Terrace and look out over the gardens and the river. Apart from giving you a chance to enjoy the view it will also allow you to read the plaques on the walls of the houses, because among others who have lived here were George Bernard Shaw, David Garrick, Charles Dickens, Thomas Hardy, John Galsworthy, Sir James Barrie, and H. G. Wells.

Turn right into the Strand, and if you are a philatelist this is your street, because in and around the Strand many stamp dealers have premises. Walk along until you come to the Savoy Hotel. Not much of this palatial hotel can be seen from the road, but it is unmistakable, with its aluminium fascia surmounted by a knight. It was built in 1889 by Richard D'Oyly Carte, and has always been synonomous with wealth and comfort. It was one of the first hotels to have a bathroom to every bedroom. And, in fact, it is built on the site of a palace — The Savoy Palace. This was built in 1245 by Peter, Earl of Savoy, the uncle of Eleanor of Provence who was the wife of Henry III. It was enlarged in 1325 into what was said to be the 'finest house in England' by John of Gaunt, Duke of Lancaster, who was its new owner. King John of France, who was captured by Edward III at the Battle of

Poitier, was imprisoned there from 1356, and indeéd died there in 1364. This fascinating house-cum-fortress was burnt to the ground by Wat Tyler in 1381. Henry VII rebuilt it in 1505 as a hospital for the relief of a hundred poor people. The only remaining part is the Chapel which although built in 1505 was much restored in Victorian times and again in 1956. This, of course, is a very convenient place for the grandest weddings to take place, as the reception can be held in the Savoy Hotel, but the women guests must be careful not to catch their heels in the cobbles on the lane outside. Among the orders of merit the Royal Victorian Order ranks fifth. This is the chapel of the Royal Victorian Order and you will find the arms of the knights on copper plates on the stalls.

Sharing an entrance with the hotel is the Savoy Theatre. It was built in 1881 by Richard D'Oyly Carte for the performance of that most English entertainment — Gilbert and Sullivan operettas. This theatre was the first building in the world to be lit by electricity.

Just a short way from the Savoy is Simpsons, where the really traditional English food is served, in the really traditional English way – Roast Beef of Olde England wheeled to your table under a vast silver dishcover. It is here that you can eat the most English dish there is, 'Bubble and Squeak', which is traditionally Sunday's left-over cold cabbage and potatoes, fried, and served with Sunday's cold meat.

As you continue your walk you will come to a bridge, Waterloo Bridge. Walk over the road at the end of the bridge, and the vast stone building confronting you is Somerset House. The original building on this site was built for the Duke of Somerset, the regent to the infant king, Edward VI, the only son of Henry VIII. He seems to have robbed innumerable buildings all over London for what must have been an enormous building. He took stone from Old St. Paul's Cathedral, from the predecessor of the present St. Mary-le-Strand, and from the Priory of St. John of Jerusalem in the Clerkenwell Road, among others. He obviously had no fear that God would punish him — but He did — because he didn't live to see his grand house finished, he was executed for high treason in 1552. So Elizabeth I lived there while her half-sister Mary I was on the throne, and here, in 1658, Oliver Cromwell lay in state. In 1776 Sir William

Chambers designed the present building in Portland stone, and it has housed, since then, various Government offices. The far end of the building is used by King's College, one of the colleges of the University of London.

In the middle of the road, at this point, is one of the hidden treasures of London, St. Mary-le-Strand, the successor to the church pulled down by Lord Protector Somerset for his stone pilfering. In 1710, the Tories passed an Act of Parliament to impose a coal tax, which would enable them to build 50 new churches in London to meet the needs of an expanding population. St. Mary-le-Strand was the first to be built, by James Gibbs in 1714, the architect of the magnificent St. Martin-in-the-Fields. Only seven others were built in the end. It is very beautiful inside, with a barrel vaulted ceiling that takes your breath away, and a pulpit by Grinling Gibbons, the master carver. St. Thomas à Becket was a lay rector of the previous church on this site, and it was in this church, in 1809, that the parents of Charles Dickens were married.

The next island of sanctuary in this sea of traffic is St. Clement Danes, a church designed by Sir Christopher Wren in 1680 but with a spire added by James Gibbs in 1719. This is the church of the Royal Air Force. Destroyed by fire-bombs in one of the last fire raids of the last war, it was lovingly restored, and reconsecrated in 1958, in the presence of Her Majesty Queen Elizabeth II and his Royal Highness the Duke of Edinburgh, who read the lesson. It has a striking interior, all white, grey and gold. A beautiful panelled ceiling in which are set the Stuart coat-of-arms, and on the floor more than 700 squadron badges made of Welsh slate, which include badges of the Commonwealth and a memorial to the Polish airmen who flew with the Royal Air Force during World War II. Under the north gallery is the American shrine, and here you will find the names of the 19,000 American airmen who lost their lives in the war flying from these shores. The pages of the book are turned every day, as are the pages of the Memorial Books that line the church, in which are written 125,000 names of the men and women who died on active service in the Royal Air Force.

The most famous children's nursery rhyme is 'Oranges and Lemons said the Bells of St. Clement's', and the bells of the church ring it out at 9 a.m., 12 a.m., 3 p.m. and 6 p.m. Since

1958, when the peal was repaired at the Whitechapel Bell Foundry where the original bells had been cast in 1693, the bells have also played the Old Hundredth and the Air Force March. Quite a carillon, so worth being near the church at midday when it is played. Towards the end of March each year, the Primary School children from St. Clement Danes primary school come to the church for a short afternoon service and afterwards are presented with an orange and a lemon each. This was Dr. Johnson's parish church, and he liked to sit in the north gallery, and watch the assembled congregation. There is a statue of him outside the church, looking down Fleet Street.

The streets to the south from this part of the Strand are reminders of Elizabeth I, because several of her most famous courtiers had large houses here with gardens running down to the river. Thomas Howard, Earl of Arundel, Surrey, and Norfolk, and Robert Devereux, Earl of Essex, are both commemorated here. The first in Surrey Street, Norfolk Street, and Arundel Street. The second in Essex Street and Devereux Court which has an attractive pub called The Devereux in it. Dr. Nicholas Barbon bought the estate from the executors of the Devereux (Robert, Earl of Essex, having lost his head in the Tower of London in 1601) and proceeded to develop it and the neighbouring properties. Unfortunately, a large amount of rebuilding has gone on here since the war, but there are still some houses dating from 1670 as well as a fairly amazing arch built at the end of Essex Street. In Surrey Street, and rather difficult to find, is a sign pointing down a little alley to a Roman Bath. The bath is a very small, only 15ft. long, and is fed by a spring, you peer at it through a window. It is situated beside a particularly pretty house called the Old Watch House.

If you walk through Devereux Court you come into Fountain Court in the Temple, but first, perhaps, a look at some of the buildings at the beginning of Fleet Street. In the centre of the road is the Temple Bar Memorial which was built in 1882 to replace Temple Bar. This was the boundary between London and Westminster and was built in 1672 by Sir Christopher Wren of Portland stone. The trouble was that it was only wide enough for two coaches to pass through the arch at a time, and therefore created traffic jams. Looking at the narrowness of the street today you will wonder if there is any improvement! No. 1

Fleet Street is Childs Bank, although now amalgamated with William's and Glyns Bank, it was one of the oldest in London, being founded in 1671. It is opposite Temple Bar, and in the Bar, over the arch, were some rooms which the Bank rented from the City Corporation.

Just a few doors along is Lloyds Bank, and it is worth poking your nose into the entrance hall, because it has the most incredible 'art nouveau' tiling. As you walk down the street you will see a timbered house. This is Prince Henry's Room, which is a large first floor room, that has connections with Prince Henry, elder son of James I. It has panelled walls and a fine decorated ceiling, and a friendly curator who answers your questions gladly.

The area around Fleet Street has always been the area of London connected with scribblers. Samuel Pepys was born there, Dr. Johnson lived there – compiling his famous dictionary in his pretty house in a courtyard a few feet off the 'Street of Ink'. But it is another profession that the western end of the street is renowned for, the law. So here, I think, through the archway under Prince Henry's Room and into the Temple.

It has a marvellously leisurely 18th century air about it, and in fact many of the buildings date from that time or earlier. Look at the doorways of the buildings, and you will see, in 18th century lettering, the names of the occupants, who are mostly barristers and judges.

The Order of the Knights Templar, from which the Temple takes its name, settled here in the 12th century and they built the round church, which still stands, in 1160. They were an order of military knights, founded in 1118 to protect pilgrims on the road to the Holy City – the romantic Crusaders! But by 1312 the Pope had suppressed the order and the property passed to the crown. In 1324 the buildings were given to the Knights Hospitallers of the Order of St. John of Jerusalem, and they were the people who first leased the ground to the lawyers. But in the Reformation the Knights Hospitallers were also suppressed, so the lawyers, who had settled there as tenants, formed themselves into two Societies – the Inner and the Middle Temple. They secured the freehold by charter from James I in 1608.

The Church and the Buttery still date from the Middle Ages.

The Hall of the Middle Temple was built in 1562, and although heavily bombed in the last war it is now restored and open to the public. In this hall many entertainments have taken place. Shakespeare is said to have taken part in a performance of Twelfth Night here. He certainly knew this area well because in Henry VI, the red and white roses were plucked from the Temple Gardens. It would be impossible to list all the famous people who have lived and worked here, but among them were Dr. Johnson, Charles Lamb, and Thackeray. Oliver Goldsmith is buried in the Temple Churchyard.

Go back into Fleet Street and walk down the street towards Ludgate Circus. You will pass Whitefriars Street on your right which was the site of a Carmelite monastery. Founded in 1241 it was dissolved by Henry VIII in 1538. Salisbury Court was once the London house of the Bishops of Salisbury, and on the wall of the Reuter building there is a Blue plaque to commemorate the birthplace of Samuel Pepys.

From the Court take the little alley which leads to St. Bride's Church. This is the 'Cathedral of Fleet Street'. It is another of Sir Christopher Wren's magnificent post-fire creations, built in 1671. It has the tallest spire of any of his churches being 224ft., but originally it was 8ft. higher. It was struck by lightning in 1764. It is this particular spire that inspired the creation of the wedding cake as we know it today. During the Second World War in 1940, it was gutted by bombs, but mostly through the generosity of the neighbouring newspapers, it was restored in 1953. This is the church that Samuel Pepys was baptised in, the parents of Edward Winslow, colonial governor of Massachusetts, were married in (the reredos is a memorial to him) and also married here, the parents of Virginia Dare, the first English child to be born in America. Samuel Richardson, the printer and author of Pamela, was buried here, as was Wynkyn de Worde, who was a pupil of Caxton and who introduced printing to Fleet Street all those centuries ago.

A famous argument raged over the spire of this church. George III and Benjamin Franklin argued as to whether the lightning conductor should be blunted (George III) or pointed (Benjamin Franklin). Benjamin won, and not only was a pointed one installed on the newly built spire – but also on Buckingham Palace! In the crypt there is an interesting exhibition showing the growth of the area, and there you can also see some Roman pavement that has recently been excavated.

The next port of call must be The Cheshire Cheese so cross Fleet Street and go westwards until you reach Wine Office Court. The Cheshire Cheese was rebuilt in 1667 after the Great Fire of London. The builders of London seem to have had their priorities right – build the pubs first to refresh the builders! This hostelry is justly famous, it is very picturesque, many of its fittings and furniture date from 1667 – and they are very generous with their portions of delicious roast beef. Dr. Johnson and Boswell are reputed to have met there, and this would not be surprising because Dr. Johnson's house is very close. So after a well earned rest, and delicious lunch, off to Dr. Johnson's House in Gough Square.

It is an attractive house, and it was built in 1700 of dark red brick. It is full of pictures and prints of the great doctor. Many of them of or by his friends like Sir Joshua Reynolds. After walking your way up through the house, it has four storeys, you come to the attic, where his Dictionary was written and is on display there for you to see.

After leaving Dr. Johnson's House walk westwards towards the Law Courts, leaving the newspaper world behind you. The pubs and cafes, which in the area we have just left, were full of journalists – and at night compositors – are now full of lawyers.

St. Dunstan's in the West, a nineteenth century church with a very interesting clock which has 'striking jacks' who come out and strike the bell, has a commemorative stained glass window to Isaak Walton. There was a much earlier church on this site but it was replaced by the present one. Isaak Walton worshipped in that church, as did George Calvert, Lord Baltimore, who founded Maryland, and Daniel Brown of Connecticut, who was the first Anglican clergyman to be ordained for America.

The Royal Courts of Justice, or the Law Courts, as everybody calls them, are on the boundary between the City and Westminster. Westminster Hall served this purpose from the time it was built in 1092 until 1882, but as the population grew so did the need for more courts, so in 1874 G. E. Street designed these and they were opened in 1882. They are a marvellous Gothic fantasy outside, and inside the Central Hall is huge, echoing, and Victorian. It has a vast mosaic floor which was designed by Street. There is a small legal costume museum off this hall, but if your feet have had enough for one day, why not go and sit in one of the courts and listen to a case. This is not a criminal court – for that you have to go to the Old Bailey, but it is still very interesting to sit and watch British justice at work. And afterwards to have a nice cup of tea in the Central Hall Cafe.

CHAPTER FOUR

Opening and Closing Times
The City

The Mansion House
Mansion House Place, E.C.4.

On written application
from the Secretary
to be viewed on
Saturday afternoon.

Guildhall
Guildhall Yard, E.C.2.

Daily 10.00-17.00
Sundays from 1st May to
end Sept. Closed Dec. 25th/26th,
1st Jan, Good Fri, Easter Monday.

Stock Exchange
Old Broad Street, E.C.2.

Mon.-Fri. 9.45-15.15

London Museum
150, London Wall, E.C.2.

Tues.-Sat. 10.00-18.00
Sunday 14.00-18.00

Lunch

The Butler's Head, Mason's Yard, E.C.2
The Bow Wine Vaults, Bow Lane, E.C.4.

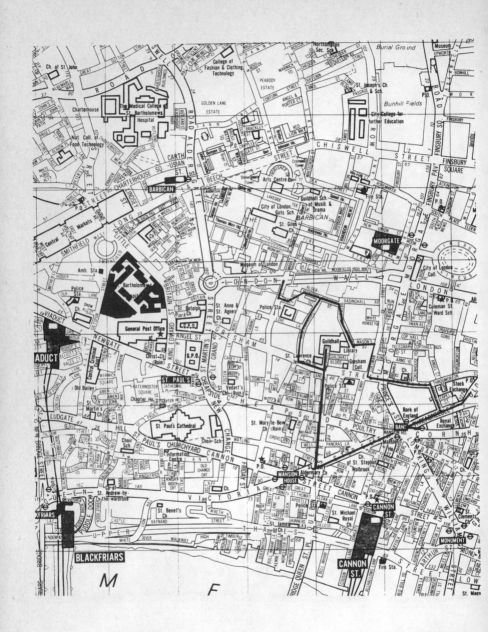

The City

Every child has heard of Dick Whittington but probably not many realise that he was a real person, born in 1388 in Pountley, Gloucestershire. The son of Sir William Whittington, he was Lord Mayor of London not once – but four times in 1397, 1398, 1406 and 1419. There is still a Lord Mayor of London. He is elected from the Aldermen of the City, who in turn are selected from the Liverymen of the City Guilds. The City Guilds are Livery Companies, medival foundations organised to look after a certain trade or craft – medival trade union in fact. There are 84 companies, many of them very prosperous. Most of the larger companies have magnificent halls. Although some were badly bombed – or disappeared altogether during the war – many have been carefully restored and rebuilt. The senior company is the Mercers' company and it was of this company that Dick Whittington was a member.

Although 'Lord Mayor' sounds very archaic, in fact he represents the power and the independence of the City of London, a fact many monarchs have had to acknowledge in the last 800 years. And the Lord Mayor's Show, on the second Saturday in November, when the Lord Mayor goes to the Law Courts to present his credentials to the Monarch's representative, the Lord Chief Justice, is one glorious, exuberant, colourful pageant, with the Lord Mayor himself riding in a coach to rival the Gold State Coach. It was actually made at the same time, and the panels were also painted by Cipriani.

Although the Mansion House, which is the official residence of the Lord Mayor during his year of office, can only be viewed on Saturday afternoons, and then only on written application to the Secretary, it makes a convenient starting place for the City. So come out of the Underground Station, or get off the bus, and you are at the confluence of eight roads. The real heart of the City, the Mansion House, is probably the prettiest of the buildings here, so let's look at it first. The site on which the Mansion House is built has many historical associations. It is the site on which the old Stocks Market stood and it is also the site of the first case of the plague in 1665, which subsequently spread all over London, killing a large number of the population. It was built in 1753 by George Dance the Elder, in the popular Palladian style, and it is made prettier by the overflowing boxes of geraniums standing between the pillars. Inside it has reception rooms that are as grand as you would imagine, with the Egyptian Hall being the grandest. It was the scene of the Lord Mayor's Banquet, during the war, when the Guildhall was damaged by bombs.

Just behind the Mansion House, down a little street called Walbrook, which was once the site of a navigable stream of that name which now runs under the pavement in a pipe, you will glimpse what appears to be a rather small, rather dirty looking church — the Parish Church of the Lord Mayor, St. Stephen Walbrook. The exterior in no way prepares you for the interior, which is magnificent. It was designed by Sir Christopher Wren in 1672-79, and like so many of the City churches it is the third church on this site — the first one dating from 1100. It has a beautiful circular dome which is supported on eight arches, which in turn are supported by Corinthian columns, and the effect is of an enormous amount of light. It is very similar to, and perhaps a model for, St. Paul's Cathedral. Most of the wealth of very fine woodwork has the usual attractive carving one expects to find in Christopher Wren's churches — everywhere there is a harvest of fruit and flowers, but most of all there is flooding light. On the north wall is a large painting by the American artist Benjamin West, of the martyrdom of St. Stephen. But probably the most important thing about this wonderful church was the founding of The Samaritans by the Rev. Chad Varah, the Rector. He, with a group of dedicated volunteers, ran this lifeline for the suicidal from the Crypt and nursed it into the worldwide organisation it is today.

After looking at this Christian Crypt, a visit to a pagan one — and in the respectable City of London too! If you go down the street called Bucklesbury when you leave St. Stephen's, and then turn left on Queen Victoria Street, you will come to the Temple of Mithras on your left. This particular street was badly bombed in World War II, and in 1954 the site was being excavated prior to the building of Bucklesbury House. During the excavation the Temple was found; and under the guidance of the Director of the Guildhall Museum the site was laid bare for all the world to see — minus the sculptures which are now in the Museum of London. The Temple was built in about 90 A.D., and although not very large, being only about 60 ft. by 20 ft., was the centre of a very important cult, founded in Asia-Minor and taken to Rome — a sort of soldiers' free-masonry through which they progressed, the emphasis being on toughness. Now looking at the remaining grey stone walls it is hard to imagine these magnificent gladiators going through their rites in a cold and alien country. This area has many Roman associations as the archaeologists discover every time they dig.

As you will see by looking at the skyline this area has an enormous number of churches, many of them built by Sir Christopher Wren after the Great Fire of London in 1666. If you cross over Queen Victoria Street and turn into Queen Street, you will see yet another Wren Church on the corner. This one is St. Mary Aldermary. It is rather different from the usual Wren churches we have come to expect in our prowls round the City because it is built in the Gothic style, with remarkable fan-vaulting. It was rebuilt (being yet again the third church on the site, the first dated 1100) under a bequest by Henry Rogers, who specified that it must be built after the fashion of the previous church, and Christopher Wren, that genius who built 50 city churches, pulled a cat out of the bag, and produced a perfect Gothic church!

As you walk down the City streets, you will see and pass many of the Halls of the Livery Companies. They are often of great historical interest, with treasures of plate and artefacts of historical association i.e., the dagger used by the Mayor, Sir William Walworth to kill the rebel leader Wat Tyler in 1381. This is in the Fishmongers' Hall. They are a very strong link with the City's past, which is also repeated in the street names around you, i.e., Bread Street, Milk Street, etc. Most of the Halls are open to the public on specified days in the year, which are announced in the press. As you can imagine, the treasures of the Goldsmiths' Hall are well worth looking at!

You are now walking towards the Guildhall, the only building left standing, but not intact, after the Great Fire of London. As you approach it in its sheltered courtyard, you will see the City coat-of-arms 'Domine dirige nos' over the medieval and fan-vaulted porch. Then you enter the Great Hall itself, which is 152ft. by 59ft. It was built in 1411-25 and this itself replaced a very much older Guildhall. As the name implies, it was a meeting place of the guilds, a place of civic assembly, where the respected citizens, who would of course be senior members of their guilds, would meet for council meetings — the running of the City. Nowadays, this hall is the place where royalty is entertained when it visits the City — a sort of neutral ground between the Lord Mayor and the State. It is the scene of banquets and receptions as well as public and municipal meetings, and this is also the site of the 'Common Hall', a most colourful ceremony, held on June 24th, Midsummer Day, when the sheriffs are elected from the liverymen for the coming year. This ceremony can be viewed if application is made in advance. Not every occasion held in this ancient hall was a happy one, because in the past it was used for important trials, such as that of Lady Jane Grey and Archbishop Cranmer.

After 1666, much rebuilding had to be done, and in 1940, in the terrible fire of December 29th when the German bombers set so much of the City alight, the roof was destroyed, but it was well restored by Sir Giles Gilbert Scott who added stone arches with a flat panelled ceiling between, as well as new panelling to the ends of the Hall and new and very effective stained glass windows which show the names and dates of all the Mayors and Lord Mayors of the City — 663 in all. If you look around the walls you will see the shields of the livery companies painted on the cornice as well as the banners of the 12 main companies. If you look to the west end of the Hall you will see Gog and Magog, two very well-known City inhabitants, two giants whose wooden predecessors lived in the Hall until 1940 when they were destroyed by the bombs. These two giants are supposed to represent the struggle between the ancient Britons and the Trojans and are carved in limewood by David Evans. To the right of the screen where the giants stand is the statue of another giant — Sir Winston Churchill. There are several interesting sculpted monuments on the walls — Nelson, Wellington, the Earl of Chathan, William Pitt the Younger, and William Beckford, the Lord Mayor in 1762 and 1769 who is remembered for giving the crown a good telling off!

The Crypt beneath the Great Hall mostly dates from 1411,

but in recent restoration work parts of the previous pre-1400 Guildhall have been revealed. The Crypt has been divided into two, is large and impressive, with Purbeck marble columns, vaulting and carved bosses.

To the east of the porch is a hall used for receptions; on the ceilings are the arms of 14 of the City Livery Companies. This was formerly the Library but that has now been moved to a new building beyond the hall. This was built in 1974 by Sir Giles Gilbert Scott. The Library is a treasure house for anyone interested in London. It contains over 140,000 books and pamphlets and over 30,000 manuscripts, as well as many prints, but, as you can imagine, it also suffered a great deal in the bombing, losing much irreplaceable material. The Clockmakers' Company also displays a collection of clocks, watches and chronometers there, a very interesting collection and a very attractive one, with some really beautiful enamelled 17th century timepieces.

When you come out of the Guildhall, turn left into Aldermanbury, and sit for a while in the garden you will see there, because this garden represents recent history. This is the site of a church called St. Mary Aldermanbury, which was rebuilt by Sir Christopher Wren in 1680-87. Unfortunately, it suffered very badly in the bombing of 1940, but this doesn't mean it no longer exists, because its walls and tower were transported across the Atlantic to Westminster College, Fulton, Missouri, where they have been incorporated into a new chapel and library in 1964 as a memorial to Sir Winston Churchill.

This particular corner of the City is rich in Livery Halls. The Brewers', Plaisterers', Pewterers', Haberdashers', and Goldsmiths' Halls all being close to where you are standing. Their use now is mostly for receptions and dinners, a thought which will probably make you feel hungry. But before you retrace your steps through the lanes and courts, walk along Aldermanbury until you see the new London, sitting beside the old. Here at the end you will see London Wall. This area was obliterated in the Blitz, and as you can see is being entirely rebuilt with high rise buildings, walkways and piazzas. At the end of this complex to the left, resembling a stone fortress, which is exactly what was on this site in Roman times, is the London Museum, one of the most fascinating museums in London, showing the growth of this great city from Neolithic to modern times. When you stand on the walkways you can see the remaining sections of the Roman Wall.

If you wend your way down the back lanes and courts you will find yourself in Mason's Yard. Here you will find a typical City pub — The Butler's Head. Like many City dining places there is a preponderance of men here, but if you are a woman don't be put off, it doesn't mean you are not allowed, it just means there are more men than women in the City. This is another pub to be described as Dickensian, and very truthfully. Dark but not gloomy, with a large bar on the ground floor. Then a Dining Room on the floor above, and on the floor above that another dining area which is a gallery to the first one. Good English food, served by jolly waitresses and very good value for money. If this type of meal does not appeal to you then walk down Lawrence Lane to Bow Lane, where you will find the Bow Wine Vaults. Good wine, of course, and nice salads. From here it is an easy walk to the Stock Exchange.

The Stock Exchange was founded in 1773, but didn't move to this site until 1802. That building was demolished in the late 1960's, and now the Exchange inhabits a 26-storey tower block completed in 1973. It contains a public viewing gallery from where you will get a very good bird's eye view onto the floor. There is plenty of free literature to hand to explain to you about the jobbers and the brokers, to tell you who wears the shiny top hats, and even to tell you when the first lady stockbroker managed to break into this male-dominated profession. There is also a cinema showing films continuously, which explains some of the finer points of dealing in, and owning, stocks and shares.

Probably no one needs to be told that the 'Old Lady of Threadneedle Street' is the Bank of England. She stands near the Stock Exchange like a well-endowed old woman in a crinoline. The massive outer wall was designed by Sir John Soane in 1788, and this encircles four acres of the most valuable land in Britain, on which stand seven storeys above the ground and three below. Most of the interior is the work of Sir Herbert Baker who reconstructed it in 1924-39, but the only part you will be able to see is the entrance hall from which you get a good view into a central courtyard, and also of the pink-coated gatekeepers.

Opposite the Bank of England is the Royal Exchange, which is a massive 19th century building by Sir William Tite, 1842-44. Sir Thomas Gresham founded the original Royal Exchange in 1565 as a centre of trading and commerce. His building was burnt down in 1838. The floor of the present building, of Turkish honeystone, is the original floor of the original building, and the 11ft. long golden grasshopper weather vane which surmounts the 180ft. high campanile is the crest of Sir Thomas Gresham and also probably original.

As you stand facing the building, on the triangular pavement, beside the statue of the Duke of Wellington, by Chantrey 1844, and the War Memorial, by Sir Aston Webb and Alfred Drury 1920, you will see it is in the classical style, with a broad flight of steps leading up to a Corinthian portico. Inside is a glass-covered courtyard where exhibitions are held from time to time. Behind the Exchange is a courtyard in which is commemorated George Peabody, who died in 1869, and is fondly remembered by Londoners for his great philanthropy. Also behind the Exchange is a charming group called 'Maternity' by Dalou and a few seats for you to stop and watch the world go by before you dive back into the Underground, or clamber onto a bus, because you are now back at your original starting point.

CHAPTER FIVE

Opening and Closing Times
Petticoat Lane

Petticoat Lane
Middlesex Street, E.1

Open all day Sunday

The Whitechapel Art Gallery
80, Whitechapel High St., E.1

Daily 11.00-5.50,
closed Saturday

The Geffrye Museum
Kingsland Rd., E.2

Tues.-Sat. 10.00-17.00,
Sunday 14.00-17.00

Lunch

The Hog Lane, Middlesex Street.
Jack the Ripper, Commercial Street.
Bloom's Kosher Restaurant, 90, Whitechapel High Street.

Tea

Geffrye Museum Coffee Shop.

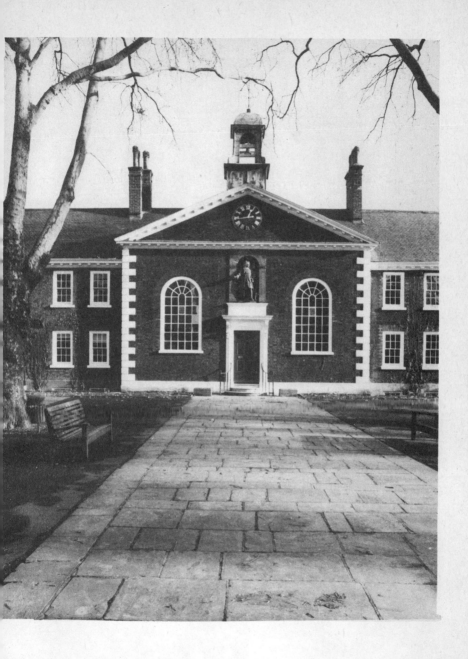

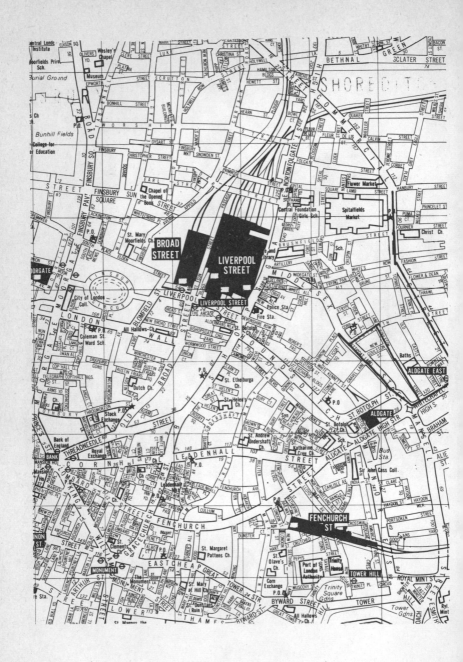

Petticoat Lane

The east end of London has always been the poor end, the area where immigrants settled, when they arrived from Eastern Europe, Ireland, or more recently Pakistan. As a result it has continued to be the poor end, because, if through industriousness and thrift, they managed to better themselves and move out to a more salubrious area, there was always a new wave of immigrants to move in. Of all the newcomers over the centuries the Jews have made the most impact, imprinting their customs indelibly to such a degree that we can't imagine it any other way.

The Jews suffered massacres and expulsion from England in the middle ages, but in the time of Cromwell they returned. In 1701, the Sephardic Jews built their handsome Spanish and Portuguese Synagogue in Heneage Lane, off Bevis Marks, and that is the oldest synagogue in use in Britain. The other Great Synagogue, which was also built in the 18th century for the Ashkenazim Jews, was in Duke's Place, but sadly this was bombed.

Petticoat Lane, which is probably the most famous street market in Britain, is just a few hundred yards to the east. Even in the 16th century Stow was writing about the houses which were 'for the most part possessed by brokers, sellers of old apparel, and such like'. But the market as we know it was started in about 1880 by the Jewish tailors of Aldgate, Whitechapel, and Mile End, to sell their wares after the Sabbath day of rest — and it wasn't just petticoats they sold. Over the last century it has expanded from its birthplace, which was Middlesex Street (Petticoat Lane being a nickname), into many of the small streets leading off it, and at Christmas time it extends over Commercial Street into the little streets and alleys on the far side making it a really enormous market.

It also sells a very much wider variety of goods than was originally intended, most things are on sale here, from the traditional pets of the East Enders, songbirds, to kitchen equipment, antique cameras, and — petticoats. It's all there somewhere. But do be warned, it is very crowded, so if you *are* looking for a specific thing it can be quite a battle to find it. Also, before you leave your starting point at the beginning of the lane, plan a meeting place, because in the crowds it is very easy to get parted, and you don't want to spoil a fun day, by panicking because you've lost one of your party!

There is also a wide variety of traders. Although there is a large preponderence of Jews, practically every other race is represented there as well. It is here that you will hear the broad cockney accent, often spoken in rhyming slang, i.e. 'apples and pears' for stairs, 'trouble and strife' for wife. The true Cockney (born within the sound of 'Bow Bells', the chimes of the church of St. Mary-le-Bow in Cheapside), has a very sharp and pungent wit. Not the sort of wit you want to get on the wrong side of, but worth stopping and listening to some of the stall-holders as they call out their wares.

As it can be so crowded, and the roads and pavement are very uneven, dress comfortably, particularly on your feet, and hold hard on to your wallet, this area is not renowned for its honesty!

There are many good bargains to be had, particularly if you are looking for a specific thing, and most of the shops around are open, so as well as walking in the road to look at the stalls, you will have to walk behind the stalls on the pavements to look into the shop windows if you want to see everything.

Perhaps you won't even bother with lunch because practically the first stall you come to as you enter Middlesex Street from Aldgate is Tubby Isaacs' Sea Food Stall. He is probably the most famous stallholder here, because he is reputed to have had his stall longer than anyone else. On it he sells the most delicious sea food — but not by any means the only sea food you will find in the lane. The Cockney's great love of cockles and whelks is well represented, but you will also find prawns, jellied eel, and anything else that has taken his fancy in the fish market at Billingsgate. So by the time you've topped and tailed and eaten a bag of shrimps or prawns as you've walked along, you might well have reached a hamburger, or hot dog, or kebab stall, so there will be your next course if you fancy it. After another few hundred yards of munching your way through whichever of the delicacies you choose, you then have your choice of vast quantities of fruit, or of course, ice-cream, as your pudding.

And finally, to wash it down, a beer or a shandy in one of the overflowing pubs, with which the street abounds, like the Hog Lane in Middlesex Street, or the Jack the Ripper in Commercial Street. Both these pubs sell lunches and snacks if you would prefer to sit down rather than eat on the hoof. Both are traditional, large, East End pubs, but sadly rather smartened up, with Dive bars in the cellars for more select drinking. The best and oldest pub in this part of the East End is the Hoop and Grapes in Aldgate High Street, very old, very dark, very traditional, and worth a detour. As you can imagine, all the pubs in the area do a roaring trade on a Sunday when the market is in progress, and everybody patronises them, not just the tourists, or the shoppers, but also the stall-holders and the porters as well, and it is not unknown for them to start a sing-song — even to the extent of some people doing 'Knees up Mother Brown!'. And at Christmas time there is bound to be a rendering of Carols!

In keeping with the Jewish aspect of the area you could lunch at Bloom's in Aldgate, one of the few, and certainly the most famous Jewish restaurant in London. They are very busy on Sundays and the service is incredibly fast because they do not Sundays and the service is incredibly fast. They do not encourage people to stay and linger over their meal because they will be trailing out of the door, but there are many family parties and there is an atmosphere of exuberance. They sell all the traditional Kosher dishes, and they are not too expensive.

It is in the hinterland here that Jack the Ripper murdered most of his victims. In the 1880's six women, mostly prostitutes, were hacked to death, and horribly mutilated, by the still unknown killer. The horrifying photographs of his victims can be seen at the Black Museum at Scotland Yard. At this time, several years after the Industrial Revolution, the main fuel available, and plentifully, was coal. As a result London suffered the most terrible, impenetrable, fogs, pea-soupers. One can imagine, only too vividly, the poor women standing, selling their wares on the streets. Then footsteps — then death at the hands of Queen Victoria's son the Duke of Clarence? Mr. Gladstone? A very eminent surgeon of the day? All people who over the century have been put forward as possibilities, but if the police do know the identity of the killer they are not telling.

In this corner of the city are some of the most magnificent churches to be found in London. Sadly some of the best of these have never been repaired following bomb damage and just sit there, empty shells, waiting for the money and the swell of public opinion to restore them. As it is Sunday here are one or two by name in case you would like to go in and view them. Beside the Underground station in Aldgate is St. Botolph's, a lovely church built by George Dance the Elder in 1744, now sadly in the centre of a traffic island, but worth taking your life in your hands and crossing to see, because there are two memorials in it that are piquant reminders of its proximity to the Tower. One is to Thomas Lord Dacre and one to Nicholas Carew, both of whom were beheaded on Tower Hill in 1538. Two of the many people who lost their heads in the reign of King Henry VIII. Daniel Defoe, the author of Robinson Crusoe was married here, and in 1747, here was christened Jeremy Bentham, the philosopher and founder of University College, London, where his fully dressed skeleton can be seen sitting in his chair! This church has a very fine organ by Renatus Harris.

Just outside this church, once stood the Aldgate itself. It was one of the five gates in the Roman wall which led into the City of London. The other gates were Aldersgate, Bishopsgate, Cripplegate, and Ludgate. Newgate and Moorgate were later additions. Most of them were demolished in 1760.

The first great poet of the English, Geoffrey Chaucer, took a lease on the house over the Aldgate in 1374. He then lived in it for eleven years. During this time he worked for the Crown as Comptroller of the Customs and Subsidy of Wools, Skins, and Tanned Hides. Also during this time he did most of his writing, including several of his stories for the 'Canterbury Tales'. He is buried in Westminster Abbey — and he must have been tiny because he has one of the smallest tombs there, in Poet's Corner.

In Commercial Street there is one of the several marvellous Nicholas Hawksmoor churches in this area. Hawksmoor was a pupil of Sir Chistopher Wren, and it was he who finished the West Towers at Westminster Abbey. This church is called Christ Church. Sadly it was badly damaged in the Blitz, but even if you can't see the interior, the exterior is worth looking at, and it is sited next door to the Jack the Ripper pub, a good lunching place.

Opposite you will see Spitalfields Market, which is a wholesale fruit and vegetable market. It was founded by Charles II, who, as we all know, had a passion for oranges! The market starts functioning at 5.30 a.m. during the week, but it isn't open on Sundays. It is quite a small market, unlike Covent Garden, but now that Covent Garden has moved out of its traditional site, and crossed the river to Nine Elms, it is no longer easily accessible for the casual viewer, so Spitalfields is the place to come to if you wish to buy larger quantities of flowers for a wedding or a party. It is very colourful and noisy. The present buildings were put up by Robert Horner in 1887.

On Sundays both the Whitechapel Art Gallery and the Geffrye Museum are open. They are both small, in fact intimate, museums, so after your exhausting morning of pounding around the pavements of the East End, perhaps you would appreciate a gentle stroll around one or the other, or even both, these museums.

The Whitechapel Art Gallery is situated beside the Whitechapel Underground Station. It was built in 1901 by Harrison Townsend. It has a very local feel about it. There are school children in blazers, and people who have come in for a rest while shopping, or to escape from the cold or the heat. It houses exhibitions of modern painting and sculpture, some rather controversial, but almost always interesting.

The Geffrye Museum is fascinating, but slightly further away. In fact, after walking all morning, perhaps it would be sensible to take a bus or a taxi. It occupies the old Geffrye Almshouses which are a charming group of 18th century houses behind iron railings, with a grass forecourt, trees, and a wonderful air of serenity about them, and the outside doesn't belie the inside. It is a small peaceful museum with rooms arranged in the styles of the day from Henry VIII's time to the present day.

You enter through a door to the left, progressing through all the rooms. Very domestic rooms. Although there is some lovely furniture, particularly in old oak, it does specialise in representing how the ordinary family would have lived. In the middle, by the main entrance doors, is a small library. Here you can have a break or read, while sitting in a comfortable chair, and when your tour is ended there is a coffee bar to offer you much needed refreshment before your journey home.

CHAPTER SIX

Opening and Closing Times
The Old Bailey

The Central Criminal Court,
The Old Bailey, E.C.4

Mon.-Fri. 10.00 onwards
Sat. 11 a.m. Tour.

St. Paul's Cathedral
Ludgate Hill, E.C.4

Daily 8-6.
Crypt 10.45-3.30, exc Sun.
same for Library, Galleries, etc.

Lunch

The Cook Tavern, Smithfield, E.C.1
The Rutland, 9, West Smithfield, E.C.1

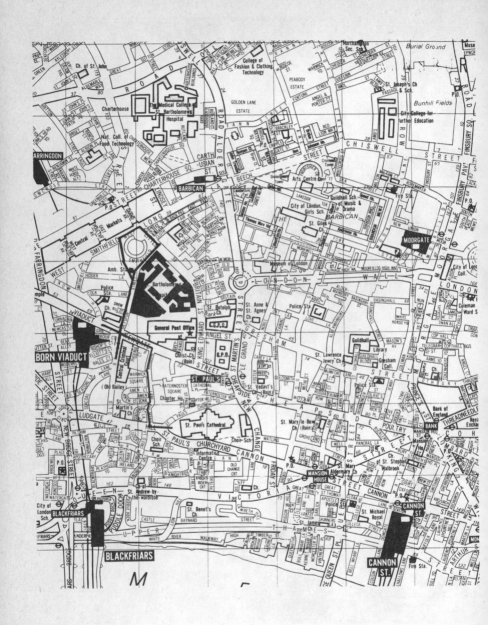

The Old Bailey

The official title of the Old Bailey is the Central Criminal Court and it is here that the criminal cases for London and some of the Home Counties are heard. The bronze figure of Justice, who stands on the dome 195ft. above the ground holding the Sword of Justice in one hand and the Scales in the other, can be seen from many vantage points around the city.

Justice was not always done here, as this is the site of Newgate Prison, the most notorious of London's prisons from the time it was founded in the 13th century until it was finally pulled down in 1902. The conditions inside it were atrocious, and many of the people incarcerated there, had, by our standards, committed very minor crimes. Jail fever was rampant and in fact Lord George Gordon, who led the Gordon rioteers in 1780, died of it while in there. Mrs. Elizabeth Fry, the great Quaker reformer, was largely responsible for the improving prison conditions in the 19th century, but in its heyday it was a noxious place.

The gallows were placed in the street outside in 1783 and one of the reasons the street is so wide at this point was to allow the crowds to watch the hangings, which were a great public spectacle.

But the spectacle we can now watch is British justice at work. There are eighteen courts at the Old Bailey and they sit at 10.15 and 1.45, so go to the Public Gallery entrance and ask the doorman which court has an interesting case, and then go in and listen. Even though the courts are now modernised, you will see the Judge, officers of the court, and barristers, wearing the traditional black robes and grey wigs. Never take your camera with you because you are not allowed to take it into the court and there is nowhere to leave it.

Afterwards cross over Holborn to St. Sepulchre Church, one of the largest city churches, which has many Newgate connections. The bells of the church tolled whenever there was an execution, and in the south aisle there is displayed a handbell which was rung at midnight on the eve of an execution outside the condemned cell — very sepulchral!

Before the gallows were placed in Old Bailey the condemned criminal was taken to Tyburn, which was on the site where Marble Arch now stands. As they passed St. Sepulchre it was the custom to present them with a nosegay — small compensation for what was about to happen to them. The history of the church dates from the 12th century. It was a foundation of the Crusaders but it was rebuilt in the 15th century and then badly damaged in the Great Fire of London. Sir Christopher Wren restored it when he was doing his great rebuilding of the city's churches.

In the south aisle, near the Newgate handbell, is buried Captain John Smith of Pocohontas fame. This church has strong musical connections. Commemorated in the north windows are Sir Henry Wood who founded the Promenade Concerts, Dame Nellie Melba, the Australian opera singer, and John Ireland, the composer. On November 22nd, which is St. Cecilia's Day, a special musical service is held here.

Although no longer standing, to the east stood a Watch Tower from where a look-out could be kept on the graveyard, as this was a very convenient source for the body snatchers who supplied St. Bartholomew's Hospital.

Another very interesting church in this area is St. Bartholomew the Great, so after leaving St. Sepulchre walk down the street beside it called Giltspur Street and you will find yourself in a large open space. Go to the east and enter a gateway under an Elizabethan half-timbered house. This house had a tiled frontage until the first world war and no one realised that behind this lay the impressive facade you see today. But an explosion from a Zeppelin bomb in 1915 loosened them and exposed it. After the Chapel in the White Tower in the Tower of London, St. Bartholomew's is the oldest church in London. It was founded as an Augustinian Priory in 1123 by a monk called Rahere, St. Bartholomew's Hospital was also founded by him at the same time. He was a favourite member of King Henry I's Court, and while on a pilgrimage to Rome he became very ill. He then vowed that if he recovered he would found this priory in London when he returned.

Although only parts of his original Norman building remain they are very impressive, with massive columns and piers and the triforium, although this is not complete, because, in the early 16th century, an oriel window was added which communicated with the Prior's house. The Prior at the time was called Prior Bolton and on the window you will see his rebus, a bolt and a tun. The apsidal east end of the choir was actually built in 1886 by Sir Aston Webb, but it is probably more in tune with the original than the 15th century replacement was.

This church suffered at the Dissolution of the Monasteries although the Hospital, which was also part of the Priory, didn't, as a result of Henry VIII's intervention. He is regarded as the second founder and his action is commemorated by a statue in a very fine gatehouse. The tomb of Rahere, who died in 1145, is on the north side of the sanctuary. It is a beautiful tomb with a richly decorated canopy over a coloured effigy. In the south transept stands the 15th century font — the only medieval font in the City — in which William Hogarth the satirist was baptised, as he was born just south of the church in Bartholomew Close.

This church seems to have served a multitude of purposes because the Lady Chapel, which was rebuilt in 1896, was once a printing office in which Benjamin Franklin worked in 1725. It subsequently became a fringe factory. In the north transept there was one a blacksmith's forge, so it had many uses other than secular. There is a charming custom that on Good Friday twenty-one poor widows receive a coin (traditionally a sixpence) from a tomb in the churchyard.

After leaving the church stroll northwards to the enormous building on the far side of the square. This is Smithfield, or the Central Meat Market, and it was built in 1867 on a very historically interesting site. It was originally Smoothfield, a large grassy expanse just outside the walls of the city, where from the 12th century it was the most important cattle and horse market of London, and also where Bartholomew Fair and many tournamants were held. But as so many sites in London it has its darker side. It was also a famous place of execution. This is where many people were burnt at the stake for their religious convictions and where the rebel leader, Wat Tyler, was slain by the Lord Mayor, Sir William Walworth, in the presence of King Richard II. In Mary Tudor's reign over 200 Protestants were burnt here.

Nowadays it is the biggest meat market in the world covering ten acres and dealing in every type of meat, poultry, and game. The lorries start arriving at 10 p.m., porters unload the carcasses, which are then cut up throughout the night and then the buyers arrive about 6 a.m. The market is at its busiest from 6 till 9 a.m. and finally closes at midday, having been thoroughly scrubbed and cleaned in preparation for the next night's arrivals. If you walk round be careful not to get in the way of a large carcass being carried on some hefty man's shoulders or you might become the victim of that typically acerbic type of cockney wit.

After looking at all that good red meat you are probably feeling hungry, so go back across the square to the Cock Tavern where you can sample some of the wares of the market, or the Rutland, where you will probably be in the company of some of the porters from the market. These are both good local pubs.

After lunch walk back down Giltspur Street to Holborn, turn left, cross over, and walk down Ave Maria Lane until you come to St. Paul's Cathedral, Christopher Wren's greatest masterpiece. The spirits soar just to look at it. It is, in fact, the sixth known church on this site, the first one being consecrated in 604 and burnt down 70 years later — a fate which befell all subsequent churches. The preceding church to the present one, Old St. Paul's, was enormous, being 596 ft. long — nearly 100ft. longer than the present one. With a steeple more than 496ft. high, it must have been a most awe-inspiring sight — but like its predecessors it was accident prone. First its steeple was destroyed by lightning in 1444, despite the efforts of the Lord Mayor and citizens to put out the resulting fire with vinegar. After the spire was repaired 18 years later it stood for another hundred years until the same thing happened again — only much more seriously because this time the whole roof was demolished. After this disaster the cathedral never retained its former glory, and although it was re-roofed it went into decline, which was accelerated at the time of the Commonwealth by the use of the Quire as a Cavalry Barracks! The nave was already known as Paul's Walk, for its use by the populace as a general market place and meeting place. In 1501 it was still grand enough for Prince Arthur, the eldest son of Henry VII, to marry Catherine of Aragon there. But by the time his nephew Edward

VI came to the Throne the church was in such a derelict state, and most of the treasure had been removed by his father, Henry VIII, that his uncle on the maternal side, Lord Protector Somerset, demolished the North Cloister to provide stones for his great palace in the Strand, Somerset House, and there doesn't appear to have been any great outcry against this plundering. The final demise of Old St. Paul's came with the Great Fire of London when all that was left standing was a very small part of the Nave.

Christopher Wren was invited to submit a design for the rebuilding of the Cathedral. After two attempts that were turned down by the Commissioners as being too revolutionary the third was accepted, but only because Charles II gave it a warrant of approval, so it became known as the Warrant Design. The rebuilding started in 1675 and the first service was held there in 1697 although it still took another 13 years to finish it.

For the next 250 years the church had a fairly uneventful time as the seat of the Bishop of London and the parish church of the British Commonwealth, until the Battle of Britain in 1940, when nearly all its precincts were totally destroyed by bombs. In 1941 it received two direct hits by high explosive bombs, one in the North Transept and one which destroyed the High Altar. Throughout the war, the vast roof was cobwebbed by ropes to enable the Night Watch, a group of volunteers, to find their way about in the darkness of the blackout. They risked their lives nightly as they scrambled over the roof clearing it of the fire-bombs as they fell on it.

As you walk into the Cathedral at the west end you will see two chapels on your left. This first Chapel is the Chapel of St. Dunstan which is used for private prayer. In this chapel above the Altar is a beautiful mosaic by Salviatti of the Women of the Sepulchre.

From here, the best way to take in the magnificence of the Cathedral, is to walk to the centre of the Nave, just inside the great West Doors, which are opened on important occasions, and gaze down at the east end. The vista is awe-inspiring, but also magical, with light and colour interplaying down its great length of 515ft. As you walk down the centre aisle notice the memorial to the Duke of Wellington on your left, with his charger, Copenhagen, on the top. At the crossing, the centre of the Cathedral, you will be under the Great Dome. The paintings, by Sir James Thornhill, represent scenes from the life of St. Paul, and in the spandrels of the Dome are brilliantly coloured mosaics by Salviatti. If you look above the spandrels and below the statues of the Fathers of the Church which are in the recesses between the windows you will see the Whispering Gallery. This Gallery can be visited by a staircase on the southwest of the crossing and it is renowned for its unusual acoustical qualities, which means that two people can stand at opposite sides of the 112ft. Dome, one can whisper something against the wall and the person on the far side will be able to hear it — great fun for children!

From beneath the Dome you can get a magnificent view into the Quire. Sir Christopher Wren was marvellous at promoting the talents of craftsmen he discovered and the Quire of St. Paul's shows the work of two of his protegés to perfection, Grinling Gibbons, the Dutch master carver, and Jean Tijou, the French craftsman in wrought iron. The woodwork in the Quire is glorious, not only on the stalls but the organ case which was built by the eccentric organ builder Father Smith in 1695. In front, and to the right of the Quire is the Pulpit which was designed by Lord Mottistone in 1963. Walk in front of the Quire to the left and down the north Quire aisle, the exquisite gates you will see are the work of Jean Tijou and more delicate tracery in this medium it would be hard to find.

Through the gates you will come to the High Altar which was consecrated by the Bishop of London in 1958 in the presence of her Majesty Queen Elizabeth II and it replaces the previous High Altar which was destroyed by a bomb. It is made of Sicilian marble decorated with wheat and grapes, with carved oak and gilt decorated columns to the magnificent Baldichino. The Altar is a memorial from the people of Britain to the men and women of the Commonwealth who lost their lives in the two world wars. In the Chapel behind the High Altar, in the apse, is the American Memorial Chapel, which contains a Roll of Honour presented by General Eisenhower in 1951, containing names of the 28,000 Americans who lost their lives in operations based in Britain in the Second World War.

In the south Quire aisle is the Lady Chapel, and after it, as you walk along, you will come to an odd memorial. It is the only memorial to come intact from Old St. Paul's and it is of its most famous Dean — the poet John Donne. His outlook was very morbid, and when he was in his last illness in 1631 he put on his shroud, closed his eyes and posed for a portrait which was given on his death to the sculptor Nicholas Stone, who created this life-size effigy.

Now it's time to visit the Crypt, which is vast, the biggest in Europe, because it extends under the whole Cathedral. Sir Christopher Wren is buried down here in the third bay on the right. It is a simple grave for so great a man, who left such an enormous heritage for us to enjoy. On the wall above his grave is an inscription composed by his son which is perfect, 'Si monumentum requiris circumspice' — if you seek his monument look around you.

Two other great men who safeguarded our heritage for us lie here but in a great deal more grandeur. First of all the Duke of Wellington lies in an immense sarcophagus of Cornish porphyry which rests on a block of granite. Next, under the Dome, the most romantic of England's heroes, Horatio Nelson, lies in solitary splendour, no Emma by his side, in one of the prettiest of sarcophagi made of black and white marble. It was originally commissioned by that great egoist Cardinal Wolsey, from Benedetto da Rovezzano, as his final resting place, but as happened to so many of his possessions when he fell from favour, it was acquired by King Henry VIII who intended it for his own use — although on looking at it one cannot imagine either of these large, well-fed, gentlemen fitting in to it. For some reason it was not used for Henry VIII and was finally brought from Windsor three hundred years later to be used by the diminutive Nelson who was brought back to England after his death at the Battle of Trafalgar preserved in a keg of rum. He was put in a coffin made from the French flagship L'Orient and finally into this last elegant resting place — a fitting end for the most famous son of Norfolk.

There is still one more extravaganza to see before we return to the light — the Duke of Wellington's funeral car, which is on show in the west end of the crypt. It is an immense, and imposing vehicle which was made from French guns and cannons captured at the battlefield of Waterloo. It took 100 men eighteen days, working in shifts, to make the eighteen ton car, and it took twelve horses to pull it, complete with the Duke, from Chelsea Hospital to his very elaborate funeral attended by fifteen thousand people in St. Paul's in 1852.

Now back up the stairs to the south transept and as you walk towards the south aisle you will see the font which was made by Francis Bird. If your feet will stand it you can climb one hundred and forty three steps to the south triforium gallery, the library, the west gallery, and the trophy room. Here you will be able to see the history of this great church in models, sketches, plans, fragments from the previous churches, and manuscripts. After another hundred and sixteen steps you will come to the Whispering Gallery, 100ft. above the floor of the church and with a magnificent view of it, and of the paintings on the Dome. A further hundred and seventeen steps will take you to the Stone Gallery which gives you a wonderful view of London. With a little more energy you could climb another hundred and sixty-six eerie steps between the inner and outer domes, up to the Golden Gallery which is at the foot of the Lantern and gives you an even more commanding view of London, then with a little extra puff, you can walk the last of the 627 steps from the floor of the church to the Golden Ball, which is at the top of the lantern.

After this enormous climb some refreshment is probably what you most need, but before you go for a cup of tea look at the painting by Holman Hunt, The Light of the World. It is a copy, but done by the artist nearly 50 years after he painted the original, which hangs in Keble College, Oxford. Near to this is the Chapel of St. Michael and St. George where you will see the banners of the Knights Grand Cross of the Order hanging above the stalls. This order is conferred on people who have given distinguished service to the Commonwealth. Like its twin chapel across the nave, the Chapel of St. Dunstan, it has a beautiful carved screen by Jonathan Mayne.

Finally, just inside the door, is the Geometric Staircase, not always on view, but very interesting when it is. Then, out of the door, down those wide stone steps, and turn to have one last look at the wonderful elevation of double columns and tower before you go to Paternoster Square to seek some refreshment.

CHAPTER SEVEN

Opening and Closing Times
Chelsea

The Physic Garden,
Royal Hospital Rd., S.W.3

Apply in writing to
The London Parochial Charities
10, Fleet Street, E.C.4

Crosby Hall,
Cheyne Walk, S.W.3

Daily 10-12, 2.15-5
Sundays 2-5.15
Ring the bell for admission

Chelsea Hospital,
Royal Hospital Road, S.W.3.

10.00-12.00, 14.00-16.00 daily.
Sunday 14.00-16.00.

National Army Museum,
Royal Hospital Rd., S.W.3

Daily 10.00-17.30,
Sunday 14.00-17.30

Carlyle's House
24 Cheyne Row, S.W.3

April to the end October
Wed.-Sat. & Bank Hol.
Mondays & Good Friday
11.00-17.00, Sundays 14.00-17.00

Royal Mews,
Buckingham Gate, S.W.1

Wed. & Thurs. 14.00-16.00

Queen's Gallery
Buckingham Gate, S.W.1

Daily 10.00-16.00

Lunch

Peter Jones Restaurant, Sloane Square, S.W.1
The Lowndes Arms, Eaton Place, S.W.1

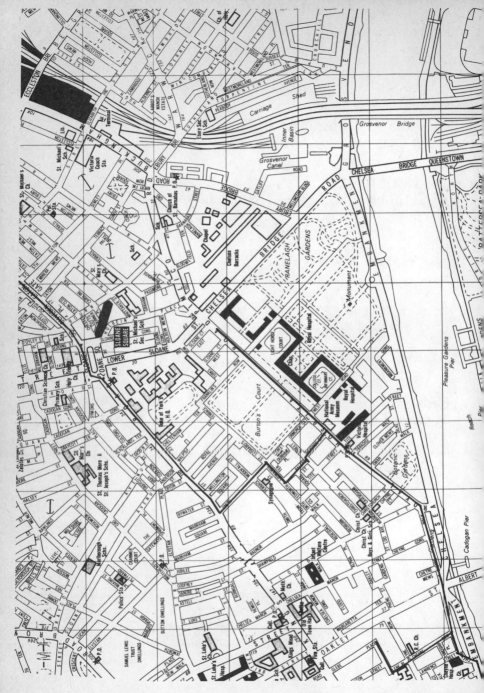

Chelsea

Chelsea is one of the oldest of the original villages in the country outside London. It was small, clustered round the 12th century church on the river, and sited between two streams that ran into the Thames. The first time Chelsea made its mark on history was when Henry VIII visited Sir Thomas More at his home there, a lovely house with gardens running down to the river, in his vain attempt to persuade Sir Thomas to change his mind about his 'great business'. After the death of Sir Thomas he acquired the manor of Chelsea and built himself a house there, where he occasionally stayed, and where the Princess Elizabeth, his daughter by Anne Boleyn, was lodged as a girl. It was also where Anne of Cleves, his fourth, and arguably most disliked (by him) wife, went to live after her divorce, and where she died in 1557. The manor was later granted by Edward VI, the young half-brother of Elizabeth, to the Duke of Northumberland, the father-in-law of Lady Jane Grey, so the unfortunate Lady Jane lived there, before she, her husband, and her father-in-law, like Sir Thomas More before them, were taken off to the Tower and beheaded.

Henry VIII and Jane Seymour, the mother of Edward VI, are said to have married secretly in Chelsea Old Church, a few days before their official wedding.

Although the church was badly bombed in the war, it has been well restored, and has many interesting memorials, which have been replaced much as they were before. There is a chapel to Sir Thomas More, who is not in fact buried there as he wished, for after his beheading on Tower Hill his head was impaled on London Bridge and finally taken down and placed in the family vault of his son-in-law, William Roper, at St. Dunstan's, Canterbury, and his body probably rests in St. Peter Ad Vincula in the Tower. There is the once magnificent, now mutilated, tomb of the Duchess of Northumberland, who, unlike many members of her family, died a natural death. There is also a brass which show the Duchess and her five daughters. The Lawrence Chapel commemorated a well-known Chelsea family, of whom perhaps Sir Thomas Lawrence, appointed secretary to Maryland in 1691, is probably the best known.

Henry James lived in Carlyle Mansions adjacent to the church and died at No. 21 in 1916. He had not been back to America for six years and when the war started in 1914 he felt he must support his adopted, and much loved country, in the only way he, an old man of 70, could. Just before he died he became a naturalised British citizen. There is a touching memorial to him.

Other distinguished people who rest in the church are Lady Jane Cheyne, a rich and benevolent benefactress, who gave her name to this area of Chelsea, and Sir Hans Sloane, who did likewise further east, and whose unique collection of flora, fauna, and geology, was the foundation of the British Museum. Sir Hans was an immensely cultivated man, the complete eighteenth century man, with all-encompassing interests. He was a President of the Royal Society, scientist, naturalist, physician, and a considerable collector of curiosities, antiquities, manuscripts, gems, and botanical specimens. His connection with one of the most famous gardens in Chelsea — the Chelsea Physic Gardens, was of great importance, particularly to Americans, because the first cotton seed in America was sent from this garden in 1732, and today three-quarters of the world's cotton crop is descended from seeds from the Physic Garden. It is the oldest Botanic Garden in England, and it is situated just a short distance away, eastwards along Cheyne Walk. It was established by the Society of Apothecaries in 1673, and in 1723, Sir Hans, who had purchased the Manor of Chelsea, and whose statue by Rysbrack (1733) stands in the garden, presented the garden to them, but with his passion for collecting he stipulated that 2000 specimens of dried and preserved plants, grown in the garden, should be sent to the Royal Society, in annual instalments of 50. Tickets to view the garden are available from the London Parochial Charities, 10, Fleet Street, E.C.4.

Another connection with Sir Thomas More is Crosby Hall, the medieval Hall to the west of the church. It was built in the City of London for a distinguished and very rich alderman, Sir John Crosby, and, after his death in 1475, it was lived in by no less a notable than the Duke of Gloucester — Richard III as he subsequently became. In 1523 Sir Thomas More brought the house, and lived there until he decided in middle age to move out to the country — Chelsea. In 1674 the house was burnt down but the hall survived. In 1910 it was moved from Bishopsgate, stone by stone, beam by beam, to rest on the site of Sir Thomas More's orchard at Chelsea. The hall is now a college hall of the British Federation of University Women, and it is open to view, just ring the bell for admission.

After all this talk of the dead, one fascinating fact emerges from the history of Chelsea, and that is its healthiness! Many people came here because the air was pure, and for asthmatics and consumptives it was considered very beneficial. It was also famous for its market gardens which grew delicious produce to be taken by cart in the early morning and sold in London.

King's Road, now famous for its shops and restaurants, was once the Royal road which led from St. James's Palace to Hampton Court Palace. After the Restoration in 1660, Chelsea became a very merry and splendid resort, culminating in the opening of the Ranelagh Gardens in 1742, with its famous Rotunda, which for a long time was the fashionable place of amusement in London, with fireworks and masquerades, regattas and balls, and where, in 1764, an eight-year-old Mozart played on the harpsichord and organ. Ranelagh Gardens is still a place to be strolled around and enjoyed, but by day rather than night. It is now genteel rather than risque, because it adjoins the Chelsea Hospital, a wonderful institution founded by Charles II, to make a home for old and disabled soldiers, called Chelsea Pensioners of whom there are 420. They are instantly recognisable because they wear very unusual uniforms, and you will pass them sitting in the gardens and walking along passages as you wander round.

The Hospital was designed by the ubiquitous Sir Christopher Wren and built in 1682-92. The Hall and the Chapel are open to the public between 10-12 and 2-4 and here you will probably find a pensioner who will act as a guide. A tip is in place here. If you wish, you could go to service on Sunday in the Chapel, which has some marvellous 17th century carving in it. The large quadrangle has a statue of Charles II in Roman costume in the centre. On Oak Apple Day, 29th May, a wreath of oak leaves is placed round his neck to celebrate his escape after the battle of Worcester in 1651, when he hid in an oak tree. On the same day the pensioners blossom into their scarlet uniforms for summer. If you wander to the railings at the far side of the courtyard you will look down on the gardens. These gardens are famous as the venue of the Chelsea Flower Show, where for four days in May, they are transformed into a very over-populated gardener's delight, with huge marquees and acres of flowers. Gardeners from all over the world flock there to view the demonstration gardens, look at the new and more efficient gardening tools available, and gaze covetously at the garden furniture, which ranges from reproduction pub furniture in white cast-iron, to wonderfully soft, squashy, chaise longues in elegant prints.

The Royal Hospital has its own small Museum which is in the Secretary's Office Block to the east of the Hospital, bordering Ranelagh Gardens. One of the most notable objects on view there is the portrait of a soldier, called William Hiseland, who served a total of 80 years in the army, and died at the magnificent age of 112!

After this very small museum, make your way westwards to a very large museum — the National Army Museum. This is a new building designed to show the growth of the Army from Henry VII's Yeoman of the Guard to the present day. There are interesting displays of uniforms, portraits — and of course, weapons. During holiday times they run projects for children from an old army tent in the yard at the back, and you will have to be careful or you bump into children walking around with cardboard reliefs decked out with sand, paint, and toy soldiers.

When you leave the National Army Museum cross Royal Hospital Road, and walk up Tite Street to the King's Road, noting Tedworth Square on the way. Mark Twain lived at No. 23 during 1896-7.

Whatever the fashion, Punk or Mod, the King's Road is the place to see it in all its glory, particularly on Saturdays when people go into pubs and restaurants to see, and be seen by, other eccentrically dressed people. This has always been the case. In the 1880's the American artist James McNeil Whistler and poet and playwright Oscar Wilde were neighbours in Tite Street. Each took great pleasure in out-doing the other, both sartorially and verbally. This area has always been famous for both writers and artists, so fashion, has, quite naturally, been one of the many facets of Chelsea society. From Charles Keene, the star cartoonist of Punch, in flapping and shabby tweeds, to John Singer Sargent, a cosmopolitan and beautifully dressed American who became the most fashionable portrait painter of the 1890's, there has always been someone unusual on view. They may not have had safety pins through their cheeks like the punks of today, but Oscar Wilde's green carnation caused just as much uproar then.

Perhaps the attraction of the river is the reason why Chelsea has, from Turner onwards, been the home of so many artists. It is a very long list indeed, but included among the most famous must be William Holman Hunt, Dante Gabriel Rossetti, and Walter Sickert. Paintings abound of Chelsea Reach, and Battersea Bridge as it looked until the turn of the century. In the Tate Gallery you can see paintings of these views by Whistler, Monet, and Turner.

Another much painted scene was Cheyne Walk. It was an attractive tree lined promenade, with the waters of the Thames lapping gently on the beach. So different from today, when even to cross the road to walk along the Embankment you take your life in your hands. The volume of traffic is enormous, the exhaust fumes overpowering, and the noise quite deafening. In gentler days it was very common to see an artist with his easel recording the scene.

Writers too gathered together, and flourished, in the gentle and bohemian air of Chelsea. The sage of Chelsea was Thomas Carlyle, whose house, at No. 24 Cheyne Row, is open to the public daily. He lived there for 47 years, and it is just as he left it — you can almost smell the pipe smoke hovering in the air, the pipe that he smoked up the chimney so that his wife Jane didn't know he had been smoking. The shortest stay by a great writer was probably three weeks. George Eliot moved into No. 4 Cheyne Walk in 1880, then died three weeks later of a chill!

The artists and the writers both frequented clubs in the area — the most famous being Chelsea Arts Club. Still going strong, in a lovely house with a superb garden, off the King's Road. In the King's Road The Pheasantry was another famous haunt of the bohemian.

When you reach the King's Road turn right and walk along

88

towards Sloane Square enjoying the shops and the scene. On the corner of Sloane Square and the King's Road is one of the nicest stores in London, Peter Jones. It was built in 1936 by a dedicated Socialist, who believed that all the assistants should be partners and share in the considerable profits. It has a luscious display of goodies, specialising in furnishing fabric and furniture, although most other things are on sale there — including lunch in the top floor restaurant, if you feel you can't walk any further until you've eaten.

After leaving Peter Jones walk under the plane trees in Sloane Square, past the attractive fountain by Gilbert Ledward, to the far side and the Royal Court Theatre. This theatre has seen the opening of many of our most avant-garde plays, notably several of the plays of George Bernard Shaw and John Osborne.

Now walk into Cliveden Place. This leads into Eaton Square, which, even with a busy main road running down the centre of it, manages to be one of the most elegant squares in London. It was developed in 1825 by Thomas Cubitt. The magnificent white stucco houses, not then split into apartments, with the mews behind, now attractive small houses, give an interesting view of the "Upstairs, Downstairs" side of London, as it was lived until comparatively recently.

If you haven't already eaten, turn left down Eaton Place, noting No. 99 as you go. This is the house in which Chopin gave his first London recital in 1848. One of the houses in this street is said to be the actual house used in the T.V. series of "Upstairs, Downstairs". Walk just a few more steps to a pub, hidden just around the corner, called the Lowndes Arms. This is a busy lunchtime pub which does a good trade in traditional pub food like cottage pie, and steak and kidney pie. Go to the counter, give your order, buy your beer, and search for a table — you may have to share. Also beware of the cat, who stalks around, deciding who he is going to sit with, and what he is going to eat!

After lunch walk back into Eaton Square, turn left and walk to the far end. Only residents have keys to the gardens so you will have to keep to the pavements. At the end of the Square you will see a huge classical church. This is St. Peter's, Eaton Square, another of the fashionable churches for weddings, partly because it is in a fashionable area, and partly because it will hold a large congregation.

Walk past the church, cross the traffic lights, you will then see the wall of Buckingham Palace in front of you. Keep walking past the cottages and follow the wall round the corner. Now you are in Buckingham Palace Road. Just a few yards along and you will come to the entrance of the Royal Mews. These are open to the public on Wednesday and Thursday afternoons, and they show the Queen's horses and carriages.

The entrance into the main quadrangle is under an imposing Doric archway which was designed by John Nash when he was redesigning Buckingham House into Buckingham Palace for King George IV in 1825. Go through the public entrance and the first thing you will see is quite magical — Cinderella's coach perhaps? It is in fact the Gold State Coach, used by the Queen on her Silver Jubilee. It was designed by Sir William Chambers in 1761, and the panels were painted by Cipriani. There are many other coaches on view, and not all are grand. Some, like the Balmoral Sociable, are small, but cosy and comfortable in the back, although cold for the driver in the front. There are also two-horse sleighs to be seen, one designed by Prince Albert, the consort of Queen Victoria, for his queen, this had its first outing in Brighton in February 1845, along the snowy London Road, with the Prince driving the Queen, and with a footman behind.

The stables must be the most perfectly kept anywhere, with, as you would expect, the most beautiful and intelligent looking horses. They are mostly Cleveland Bays, and Windsor Greys, with names like Canberra, Philadelphia, as well as George and Buttercup.

After the stables there are displays of the gifts given to various members of the Royal Family on their tours abroad, such as the Mexican saddle presented to H.R.H. The Prince of Wales by Col. Jim Cody.

After you leave the Mews, if you still have some energy, you could continue walking along Buckingham Palace Road towards the front of Buckingham Palace until you come to the Queen's Gallery. This was once part of the private chapel of Buckingham Palace. It was badly bombed during 1940, but was restored and was opened in 1962 as a small gallery, designed to show a sample of the Royal Art Collection. The exhibition changes about once a year, and as the Queen has the most wonderful collection of pictures and drawings, started by Charles I, you will spend a very rewarding hour walking round it.

CHAPTER EIGHT

Opening and Closing Times
Bloomsbury

Dickens House 48, Doughty Street, W.C.1	Daily 10-12.30, 14.00-17.00. Not Sundays or Bank Holidays
Thomas Coram Foundation for Children, 40, Brunswick Square, W.C.1	Mon. to Fri. 10-12, 14.00-16.00. Not Bank Holidays
Courtauld Institute Galleries, Woburn Square, W.C.1	Daily 10-17.00 Sundays 14.00-17.00
Percival David Foundation of Chinese Art 53 Golden Square, W.C.1	Mon. 14.00-17.00 Tues. to Fri. 10.30-17.00 Saturday 10.30-13.00 Not Sundays & Bank Holidays
Wellcome Historical Medical Museum, 183, Euston Road, W.C.1.	Daily 10-17.00. Closed Sundays & Bank Holidays.
Jewish Museum, Woburn House, Tavistock Square, W.C.1	Mon.-Thurs. 12.30-15.00. Sundays 10.30-12.45

Lunch

Brunswick Centre, W.C.1.
The Friend in Hand, Herbrand Street, W.C.1

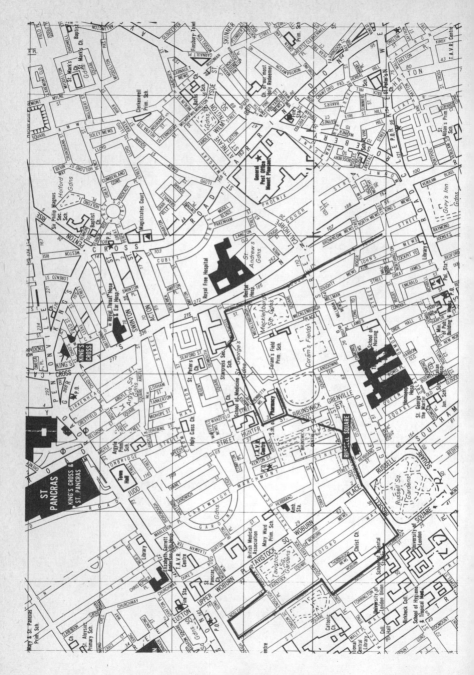

Bloomsbury

For many people London is the London of Charles Dickens. He has, through his books, created an indelible impression of a city, slightly sleazy, very smoky, but also very much alive. Even Londoners find themselves describing things and places as very Dickensian. Although his parents were married at St. Mary-le-Strand in 1809, he was born in Portsmouth in 1812 where his father was a clerk in the navy pay office. In 1814 his father was transferred back to London. But in 1821, due to Admiralty reforms, he lost his job. After struggling for several months to keep the family in the little house in Bayham Street in Camden Town in which they lived, he was arrested for debt and put in the notorious Marshalsea Prison in Southwark. Poor Charles, who was only 10 at the time and very small for his age, had to go and work in a blacking factory in Hungerford Market, which was four miles from Bayham Street, a distance he had to walk twice a day! Eventually he found lodgings in Lant Street, which was very close to the Marshalsea, to facilitate visiting his father, which the poor little boy had done on Sundays — his one day off, trudging, yet again, all the way from Camden Town. After his father's release from prison to take a job as a journalist, young Charles managed a few years of school, at the Wellington House Academy in the Hampstead Road, but it *was* only a few years, because at 14 he was working as a solicitor's clerk in Gray's Inn, and spending any free time he had at the British Museum to widen his reading. At 17 he copied his father's example and became a reporter. By 1836 he was becoming more successful. Several of his stories had been published in magazines and he had received £150 for the publication of the 'Sketches by Boz'. So he celebrated by getting married, at the newly-built and fashionable church of St. Luke's, Chelsea, to Catherine Hogarth, the editor's daughter.

The year after he was married he moved to 48 Doughty Street, W.C.1, and although he subsequently lived in many other houses, and as he became richer they became grander, this is the one that is preserved as the Dickens Museum. It was here he wrote probably his most famous book 'Oliver Twist' as well as the 'Pickwick Papers' and 'Nicholas Nickleby'. As it is open from 10-12.30 and 2-5 (not Sundays or Bank Holidays) why not start the day here?

It is a red-brick eighteenth century house in a terrace of similar houses, and inside it is full of Dickensiana — letters, manuscripts. In the basement is a reproduction of the 'Dingley Dell' kitchen, and among many pieces of his furniture, is the most important, his desk.

It is like many London houses of this period, with entrance hall and two rooms on the ground floor, and three rooms on each of the three floors above. Fine for Dickens when he was first married with only one small son, but as two daughters came in quick succession, and as financially things continued to improve, after just two years in this little house, he and his wife Catherine had to look for a larger house, and found one at 1, Devonshire Terrace. This house is now demolished, but the keystone over the front door was rescued and is now in the garden here, as you will see if you look out of the window of the Morning Room.

He loved amateur theatricals, sports, and games, and there is much evidence of this jolly side of him in the house. In the dining room is an announcement of Christmas Sports, which were held on Boxing Day 1866, and organised by him — great fun they sound too. And upstairs are several photographs and playbills of performances by the Dickens Dramatic Company; apparently he was not only a very good actor but also director and stage manager as well.

After leaving Dicken's House, your next port-of-call is exactly the type of institution Dickens might have written about, and certainly visited — the Foundling Hospital. But don't be alarmed, you won't be looking at dirty and starving urchins in a bare and freezing hall as in 'Oliver Twist'. Captain Thomas Coram was a seaman who went to sea at 11, and who, at 25, started a shipyard in Massachusetts. In 1732 he was made a Trustee for the Settlement of the State of Georgia, and even after his return to England he had very close connections with the American Colonies. When he returned he was appalled at the conditions that many children lived — and died — in, often

95

abandoned by their parents, or more often, their mothers, because many of them were illegitimate.

He set to work to collect together a group of people with influence enough, and compassion enough, to do something about it, and in 1739 opened a home in Hatton Garden. The first premises, which were not very large, were soon overflowing, so he, and his fellow Governors, were forced to find a bigger and more permanent solution. Eventually, they bought Lambs Conduit Fields from the Earl of Salisbury, and built a large hospital on the site which could accommodate many more children. But they still had to work a selection system because so many mothers brought their infants there, and after they applied for, and received, Government help in 1756, they were inundated. The condition Parliament made for giving financial help was that no one should be turned away from the doors. They took in 15,000 in the next four years and the conditions became impossible. After that, they were allowed to revert to a system of selection.

In 1926 the foundation sold the estate in Bloomsbury and the children were moved to a home in the country. The hospital was pulled down, so all that is left of the original buildings are some lovely Georgian colonnades of 1745. But continuing its association with Thomas Coram and the Foundling Hospital, the site is now called Coram's Fields and it is a play-ground, open from 9 a.m. until dusk, where adults are not allowed unless accompanied by a child.

So, unless you have someone young with you, look through the railings, and think of the vision of this one man who must have saved the lives of so many children. Now walk past London House, which is a hostel of London University and a collegiate centre for men students from abroad. Turn left down the continuation of Doughty Street. One of the interesting things to note in this street is that several houses still have the ironwork complete round their front doors, with the lamp bracket still intact. Walk into Mecklenburgh Square, which, although badly bomb damaged in World War II has, undeniably, the most magnificent houses in Bloomsbury. This, and Brunswick Square to the west, on the far side of Coram's Fields, were laid out in 1790, in the grand manner. This terrace of houses is virtually all that survives.

Go to the north side of the square, and as the road takes a turn right into the Gray's Inn Road, you will see to the left an alley with gates at the end. This is one of the entrances to St. George's Gardens, a delightful, tree-filled, hidden garden, which was once the cemetery of St. George's, Queen's Square. It has 18th century table tombs in lovely grey stone, well-kept grass and flower beds, winding paths, and seats, on which there are always people sitting even on the coldest day, and in the air there is often a smell of burning leaves as a gardener builds a bonfire in a discreet corner.

Take the path going west, stroll along it enjoying the tranquil atmosphere, and go out of the gate that is beside the little lodge cottage. This street is called Handel Street — and it is named after the musician. He had many connections with this area, one of which you are now about to see. So continue walking to the end of Handel Street, then turn left, walk to the corner, and turn left again. You are now in Brunswick Square, and there, in front of you you will see Captain Coram, in bronze, sitting in front of the offices of his foundation. Ring the door bell, you may wander round at will, looking at the magnificent and unusual art collection. And it is unusual, because among his friends Thomas Coram numbered Hogarth and Handel, Hogarth being one of the original Governors of the Foundation. In fact, due to his influence, the Hospital can claim to be the direct ancestor of the Royal Academy, because Hogarth organised some of his friends into presenting works of art to the Hospital to attract the public in to see them — and at the same time also the children — and therefore contribute to its upkeep. This became a fashionable London event, when the public wandered through the Court Room and the Gallery, rather like the present day Summer Exhibition at the Royal Academy. The Court Room and Gallery, which are very fine rooms, are still here, although the building of which they were a part no longer stands, because when it was pulled down they were taken out intact and built into this one.

The first painting in the collection was a painting by Hogarth of Thomas Coram, but another of Hogarth's pictures is in the lobby to the Court Room. It is 'The March of the Guards to Finchley'. Hogarth always felt he was underpaid for his work so with this particular painting he organised a raffle. Some of the tickets remained unsold so he gave these to the Hospital — and it won! This painting is of a typically Hogarthian scene. 'The Guards lurching drunkenly to Finchley' might be a more apt title!

There is a third Hogarth in the Court Room. It shows Moses being presented to the Pharaoh's daughter. In front of the window are some showcases containing tokens, small trinkets, a poignant reminder of those mothers who had no option but to leave their babies here, in the days before receipts were issued. One of the rules was that the babies' names should be changed when they were accepted as inmates. They *had* to have names, so the Secretary gave them any name he could think of, and these of course, were often the names of famous people — William Shakespeare, Francis Drake!

In the Picture Gallery is a Raphael Cartoon, the tapestry of which is in the Vatican, and it is here you will come across the connection with Handel. He became involved with the Hospital when the Governors were trying to raise money for the building of the Chapel. He presented the first organ, and then gave many performances, including the first performance in England of "The Messiah". He also organised the choir, and as you can imagine this turned the Chapel into one of the fashionable places of worship, and among those who regularly attended divine service here was Charles Dickens. The keyboard of that first organ is in the Picture Gallery, as is an original score of "The Messiah", which was left to the Hospital in Handel's will.

On your way up, you may have noticed the particularly fine staircase. As you go down again, look at the bannisters and see if you can see the places where there were spikes sticking up, because the staircase came from the boys' wing of the old Hospital when it was pulled down. The spikes were put there to stop boys sliding down the bannisters!

After leaving the Coram Foundation look at the enormous building on your right. This was put up in 1972, and is loved by some and hated by many, but in the piazza in the centre, there are several restaurants and cafes, so for your lunch you have a choice of Chinese, Indian, Italian — or even English food! Of if you would prefer a pub lunch take the small turning called Herbrand St., and go to the Friend in Hand, a bustling friendly pub.

After lunch walk westwards through Russell Square, one of the most famous of the Bloomsbury Squares — and also the second largest in central London. This square has many medical connections, the Royal Institute of Chemistry and the Pharmaceutical Society are both in the square. The Pharmaceutical Society has an interesting museum, the Museum of Pharmacy, in the building. But this was once a very exclusive residential area, and among the people who have lived here is Ralph Waldo Emerson, the American poet, who stayed at No. 33 when he visited England in 1833, and another poet, and indeed another American with connections in this square is T. S. Eliot, who stayed at No. 24. Dominating this area is a grey stone, temple-like building on the west of the square. This is the Senate House of the University of London, and this area, Bloomsbury, is the centre of the University — although many of its departments are housed in buildings all over London, far removed from this central area.

Bloomsbury is also famous for its literary associations, because it was the centre of the 'Bloomsbury Group', that intense group of intellectuals who lived and visited here in the early years of this century. With Virginia and Leonard Woolf, Vanessa and Clive Bell, E. M. Forster, Lytton Strachey, and J. M. Keynes all living in this area, it became a natural centre for writers.

In the north west corner of the square is the entrance to Woburn Square, a narrow square, which has been much pulled about by the University's insatiable need for more buildings. There is here, one of the most delightful small museums of modern art — the Courtauld Institute Galleries. So brave the lift, because it is on the top floor, and spend an enjoyable hour here, looking at pictures like Manet's 'Bar at the Folies Bergère', pictures you've seen so often in postcards that it's like meeting old friends when you come face to face with them.

To the left, on leaving the Courtauld Galleries, you will see, at the entrance to Gordon Square, the University Church of Christ the King. Built by Raphael Brandon in 1853, it has a very fine interior and is the principal Anglican church to London University. Gordon Square, like so many of the Bloomsbury Squares, has strong Bloomsbury connections, No. 46 having been the home of Vanessa and Virginia Stephen, before their marriages to Clive Bell and Leonard Woolf respectively, and No. 51 was the home of Lytton Strachey. No. 53 is now the home of the Percival David Foundation of Chinese Art. This is a particularly fine and important collection of Chinese Ceramics collected by Sir Percival David, and given by him in 1950 to London University, complete with this library. Every dynasty from 960 onwards is represented — Sung, Yuan, Ming, and Ching — and this small gallery, like the Courtauld Institute, is often fairly deserted, making it pleasant to wander round at one's own speed.

This is an area where most interests are catered for. If Chinese porcelain is not for you, then maybe the Wellcome Foundation, at No. 183, Euston Road, will be more your cup of tea. Here they have a museum of medical history and science, the Wellcome Historical Medical Museum, Among its many interesting contents is George Washington's medicine chest. But if this is still not for you, perhaps you would prefer the Jewish Museum which is in Woburn House, in Tavistock Square (but entered from Upper Woburn Place). This museum has an interesting assembly of antiquities and ritual objects. But this last visit of a long day takes us right back to the first, because the previous house on this site was called Tavistock House and it was lived in, from 1851-60, by Charles Dickens! In this house he wrote Bleak House, Hard Times, Little Dorrit, the Tale of Two Cities, and part of Great Expectations. And this was his last house in London, so we can't follow him any further, because in 1860 he moved to Gad's Hill in Kent, where he died in 1865. He is buried in Poet's Corner in Westminster Abbey.

CHAPTER NINE

Opening and Closing Times
Kensington

Kensington Palace	Daily 9.00-17.00 Sundays 13.00-17.00
Kensington Gardens, W.8	Sundays
Serpentine Gallery, Kensington Gardens, W.2.	Daily 10.00-17.00
Victoria and Albert Museum Cromwell Road, S.W.7	Daily except Friday 10.00-18.00 Sunday 14.30-18.00 Not Dec. 24/25/26. Good Friday
Science Museum, Exhibition Road, S.W.7	Daily 10.00-18.00 Sunday 2.30
Geological Museum, Exhibition Road, S.W.7	as above
Natural History Museum, Cromwell Road, S.W.7	as above

Lunch

Geale's Fish Restaurant, Farmer Street, W.8.
The Serpentine Restaurant, Hyde Park. W.2.

103

Portobello Road and Kensington

It is always difficult to get something for nothing, and certainly as far as bargains are concerned Portobello Road is not the place to try, but on Saturday mornings it does have one thing for free — and in abundance — carnival atmosphere. As you come out of Notting Hill Gate Underground station you will join a river of people — a tide pouring down the hill to the market, a walk of about a quarter of a mile.

As you walk down Portobello Road you will see large crowds gather to watch an escapologist doing his Houdini-like act — escaping from ropes, and chains and sacks, into which he has been locked by his accomplice. On another corner you'll see a one-man-band, beating his drum, banging the cymbals, and blowing a horn, all at the same time. Further on, a man with a monkey and a barrel organ is playing a rollicking tune. All the streets around have some peripheral activity to do with the market, perhaps a really good pub where the customers are sitting outside drinking their beer and watching the world go by, a restaurant which although small is renowned for its good cooking, with perhaps a couple of tables in a garden under a sycamore tree, or a yard, piled high with furniture and some lusty man stripping the paint from chests and dressers, for later sale round the corner in one of the emporiums.

Portobello Road starts at Pembridge Road and runs down the hill. At the top the barrows are crammed with antiques, bric-a-brac, the contents of granny's attic, but further down the street they become food stalls. Fruit and vegetables, piles of eggs and fish. At the top of the hill the shops beside the barrows are fascinating caves, filled with brass, old army badges, stripped pine, hat pins — anything! But further down they become butchers, bakers, iron-mongers (the candlestickmakers do exist but they are in the little streets at the side).

Anyone can hire a barrow from the local council for a day and sell the entire contents of their garage, garden shed and attic. On the whole the dealers are very knowledgeable about their chosen subject, and many of the subjects are fairly esoteric, such as cut-glass door handles. You are unlikely therefore to get a bargain — what you might get is something fairly unusual, and a great deal of pleasure looking.

The best way to explore all this is to walk down one side of the street and up the other, stopping if you wish to have a pint of beer in one of the aforementioned pubs.

If you continued walking down the road you would come into a hinterland that is renowned for its poverty and dilapidation, but as property prices rise, and as the young middle-class can't afford to buy houses in their traditional areas, they are gradually moving in here. It's surprising how quickly a whole street revives once one house is rehabilitated and painted and has a few geraniums round the door.

After reaching the top of Portobello Road, return up Pembridge Road to Notting Hill Gate. This is another cosmopolitan area of London, with an atmosphere of gaiety. It has a large floating population — bed-sitter land — with students and itinerants living in rooms in the large houses you pass in Pembridge Road and the other streets north of Notting Hill Gate. South of the main road is Campden Hill, a very smart area with small artisans' cottages converted into fashionable homes at the bottom of the hill, with the houses getting larger and grander as you climb up. At the top they are very grand indeed. In the 17th century this was a famous spa, and although not used, the springs are active today.

One of the few fish and chip shops you can actually eat in is in Farmer Street, just 50 feet south from the main street on the edge of the hill. You could be traditional and eat them from the paper if you prefer, but for those who don't want sticky fingers there is a restaurant. It is called Geale's, and the fish and chips are excellent.

Now return to Notting Hill Gate and turn right, passing two very good cinemas, one of which was built in 1898 as a theatre. Among the stars of the stage who played there was the incomparable Sarah Bernhardt. After you have walked along the pavement about 200 yards and crossed two roads, you will come to the gate at the end of Kensington Palace Gardens. No traffic is allowed through unless it has legitimate business here, but as a pedestrian you are welcomed. You will see a policeman standing here, because this is where several embassies are located, including the Russian Embassy. There is often a demonstration taking place at this gate, and on Sundays it is common to see a protest march with banners and chanting.

At weekends the railings on this side of Hyde Park and Kensington Gardens are used as an outdoor art gallery. All the way along artists display their work in the hope of making a sale. Even if you have no wish to buy, walk along, enjoying the colourful free show, not only of pictures, but leatherwork and metalwork as well.

This road is called Bayswater, and as the name suggests, there are springs here, which, with the aid of the stream of West Bourne, helped to create the Serpentine, the lovely lake in the park. The large and imposing blocks of houses overlooking the park were built about 1850. Although once family houses they are now mainly converted into hotels.

The street which cuts into Bayswater, halfway along, is called Queensway. A multi-national street, with late night food shops and restaurants — but best of all an ice rink. It is the only ice rink in the centre of London and it is possible to hire skates.

Enter the Park at Marlborough Gate. You will be surrounded by Londoners taking their dogs for a walk, nannies pushing their charges in prams, and children flying kites or roller-skating. It is a park that is much loved and used. You will soon come to the Water Garden which is one of the most delightful places in the entire park — very Italianate, it is a symphony in grey stone, marble and water, with children and ducks running under the spray of the fountains to keep cool on hot days. Close by is Queen Anne's Alcove, a charming brick building in which to rest.

In the Park there are many pleasant walks, the most famous being the Broad Walk which leads to the Round Pond, but if you return on the North Walk, to the west of the Lancaster Gate, you will pass the Dogs' Cemetery. This is a special cemetery for dogs founded by one of the sons of Queen Victoria, the Duke of Clarence, in 1880. After the death of his wife's dog it was interred here, as were subsequently many more, with their own tombstones, often with heart-rending inscriptions on them, and occasional posies laid on the graves — all very British.

Another landmark inside the park is the children's

106

playground, and, of course, the Elfin Oak. This is a tree stump, fantastically carved with elves and fairies. As this park has so many connections with Peter Pan and his originator J. M. Barrie it comes as no surprise to find that the swings were given by Sir James.

Afterwards retrace your steps and walk down Kensington Palace Gardens, looking at all the different architectural styles, this is nicknamed Millionaires Row — although most of the millionaires have been superseded by embassies. Kensington Palace Gardens were once the vegetable gardens to Kensington Palace, but in the 1840's this very ornate row of mansions was built in the many different styles that were fashionable in the High Victorian period. The architects were Smirke and Decimus Burton. Half way down Kensington Palace Gardens on the left is Kensington Palace.

Kensington Palace is one of the most attractive buildings in London. This is partly due to its architecture, Sir Christopher Wren again, and partly to its position on the western edge of Kensington Gardens, with its own small garden immediately around it, and beyond that, informal openness. This is why there is a palace here. William III suffered from asthma, so in 1689 he decided to buy Nottingham House and 26 acres of garden from the Earl of Nottingham and then he had it enlarged and improved on by Sir Christopher Wren. He now had a beautiful, but modest-sized palace, sitting in open country.

Queen Caroline, the wife of George II, was a very keen gardener, so when she lived there she had the 275 acres of Kensington Gardens laid out by Bridgeman, including that children's joy, the Round Pond.

The State Apartments have some fine rooms by Wren with carvings by Grinling Gibbons and some really splendid pictures. The King's Grand Staircase has attractive ironwork by Jean Tijou and wall paintings by William Kent. Kent also designed some of the rooms, which are very grand, but the most interesting rooms are those used by Princess Victoria before her accession; they have all the delight of a Victorian childhood about them.

After the Palace stroll to the Round Pond and look at the flotilla that will probably be floating on it. Dogs and boys rush around the Pond, the boys trying to turn their yachts round for open water again, and the dogs barking and splashing with excitement.

Walk down the Broad Walk until you come to the Floral Walk. This is perhaps at its best in the spring when all the bulbs are flowering — but even in the depths of winter it is a joy to walk along this well tended walk. Here you will see people who obviously come every day to feed the birds — they seem to have a name for every one!

You are aiming for the Albert Memorial which you will see ahead of you through the trees. It is a marvellously dotty Victorian-Gothic monument to that industrious, enterprising, and multi-talented German prince, who worked so hard to educate and inspire the English. You will see that he is facing south with a book on his lap. The book is the catalogue of the Great Exhibition for which he was largely responsible, and which was held here in 1851. He is looking in the direction of the land that was bought with the proceeds of that exhibition, which, with his usual thoroughness, he used for the purposes of education and improvement. Gore House, the home of Lady Kensington, was purchased in 1856 for £300,000 — property values were high in this area even in those days, but they did get 120 acres of land with the house. It was intended to be a cultural centre, and this intention has become fact just as Prince Albert wished because many of the great London museums are sited in this area.

Opposite the Albert Memorial is the Albert Hall, also in memory of Queen Victoria's beloved Albert, but totally different in style. The memorial, designed by Sir Gilbert Scott in 1872 and considered by him to be his most important work, is highly ornate, highly coloured and magnificent. 175ft. high, it dominates the trees around it. The Hall on the other hand is tremendous, and solid, and monumental, in an unusual shade of dull pink. This was designed by two officers of the Royal Engineers, Captain Fowke and Major-General Scott, and it was finished in 1871. It holds 8,000 people and is used for so many different events, that during the year there must by something for everyone to attend. There is every type of music, wrestling, boxing, beauty contests, and the famous Promenade Concerts. It is open to the public if no rehearsal is in progress.

Now go north from the Memorial into the Park. Take one of

the walks to the right until you come to the Serpentine Gallery. This was built in 1908 as a tea house, and was only comparatively recently converted to its present use, which is as a gallery of the avant-garde. It is a beautiful gallery to stroll round, even if the paintings are not to your taste — it feels more like a rather grand summer house.

When you walk down the path you will see the Serpentine Restaurant ahead of you. It is perched on the edge of the lake, with lovely views over the lake. There is a snack bar as well as the restaurant, so if you wish you could have a quick snack and carry on walking. Alternatively you could have a large sleep-inducing lunch, which might be quite a good idea if the day is hot because you could then hire a boat, from the kiosk on the far side of the lake, row into the middle and snooze for the rest of the afternoon.

While you are at the restaurant take a look at the bridge that spans the Serpentine. It is one of the most attractive in London and it was built in 1818 by the Scottish bridge builder George Rennie. If you walk across it pause to look at the views both up and down the lake and the spires of the surrounding churches. West of the bridge, the Serpentine becomes the Long Water, and it is on the bank here that you will find Sir Gilbert Frampton's famous statue of Peter Pan — it is supposed to be on the spot where Peter Pan first landed from his home which was on the island you will see in the middle of the lake. It is a place of pilgrimage for countless children. The Serpentine has always been one of the favourite spots of Londoners for swimming and boating, and in the very infrequent cold winters, skating.

If you wish to continue with your walk go south from the lake. You will cross a soft sand road, this is called Rotten Row and it is for the use of horses and riders. The name originates from Route de Roi, the King's Road to Kensington Palace. The Knightsbridge Barracks is facing you and you will often see cavalry horses being taken onto Rotten Row for exercise, as well as other riders who hire horses from the livery stables in the mews nearby. It is this area that was the fashionable place to see, and be seen, driving your carriage in Georgian times. Every day the parade took place, up and down, carriage and landaus, and dashing young men on horseback.

The Knightsbridge Barracks was built in 1970 by Sir Basil Spence and it houses the Household Cavalry. It is from here, every day, that the change of guard for the Horse Guards sets out for Whitehall at 10.30.

Now you have a choice, an afternoon spent browsing round Harrods, and the Scotch House, or an afternoon spent browsing round museums. If you choose Harrods, walk eastwards from the Barracks until you come to the statue 'Pan' by Sir Jacob Epstein. This was his last work, being completed in 1959. Turn under the arch, Albert Gate, and cross the road. You will find yourself at Scotch House. Have a good afternoon's shopping and tea in Harrods.

If you choose a museum, walk due south from the restaurant to the main gates of the park. Cross into the wide street facing you — Exhibition Road. Down this road you will find the great museums of South Kensington, the Science Museum, Geological Museum, the Natural History museum, and best of all the Victoria and Albert Museum. They are all treasure houses, all worth every minute you can spare to spend in them, but if you only have time for one, I think it should be the Victoria and Albert, that most English of Museums. It is far too vast for more than a sample tasting at a time. Like the British Museum, your whole holiday could be spent going slowly round the fascinating galleries. They often have special exhibitions on so walk to the end of Exhibition Road and turn left into Knightsbridge. The main entrance is there and you will also see what exhibitions are on.

If, however, you choose the Science Museum, you will find it halfway down Exhibition Road on the right. Don't be put off by the name Science which sounds daunting — this museum isn't — it's fun, and if you have children with you it is the ideal children's museum. Attached to the Science Museum is the Geological Museum, which you reach through a covered way inside the Science Museum.

If the dice should fall for the Natural History Museum, walk to the end of Exhibition Road and turn right. The entrance to the huge building is about 100 yards along. This is fascinating, particularly its comprehensive collection of extinct mammals, birds and reptiles.

Whichever museum you choose for your afternoon's browse, you can thank the Prince Consort for his foresight in acquiring the land for this particular purpose in the first place.

CHAPTER TEN

Opening and Closing Times
The Tower of London

The Tower   Mar.-Oct. Mon.-Sat. 9.30-17.00
                                      Sunday 14.00-17.00
                   Nov.-Feb. 9.30-16.00. Not open Sundays
Closed Dec 24/25/26, Good Friday, May Day Bank Holiday

H.M.S. Belfast   11-17.50 Daily March-Nov.
                                 11-14.30 Daily Nov.-March.

Lunch

Lion Restaurant in the Tower
Dickens Inn in St. Katherine's Dock

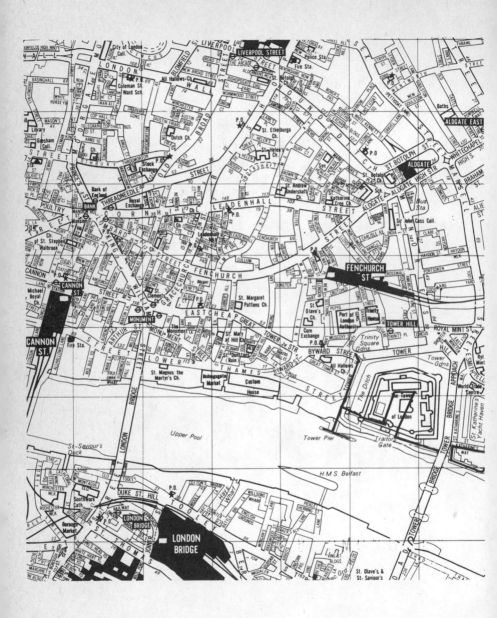

The Tower of London

When William the Conqueror landed in England, his position was very unsure and very unsafe. Although Edward the Confessor had always led him to believe he would inherit the Throne of England, on his death bed Edward named Harold as his successor. William decided to claim what he considered rightfully to be his and landed near Hastings on 14th October 1066, killed Harold, and claimed the Throne. He then had to quell a rebellious population.

He appears to have been a very organised man and a good soldier because one of the first things he did was to institute the building of defensive forts or castles every 20 miles or so. This was a day's march for his soldiers, so if there was any insurrection he could send for replacements from the next castle and they would arrive in a day. The one he built in London, which he built adjoining the Roman wall of the city, we all know — the Tower of London. He brought a monk called Gundulf over from Normandy to build it for him. Gundulf later became the Bishop of Rochester. Duke William actually built the most distinctive part, the White Tower. He brought stones from Caen in Normandy and whitewashed the finished fortress. It must have looked immensely impressive, standing there, gleaming white and very tall, when the Saxon dwellings all around were tiny hovels.

Subsequent kings enlarged and strengthened the Tower, notably Henry III who was a prolific builder, having been responsible for Westminster Abbey and a great deal of building at Windsor. He turned the Tower into a fortress, adding the inner curtain wall and many of the towers. Then the outer curtain wall and moat were built by Edward I. The whole covers eighteen acres.

Edward I was right in providing this extra protection because over the centuries the prisoners who have lived and died here make a very long list indeed — and a very gory one. The first known prisoner is the man who completed the first stage of the building Ranulph Flambard, Bishop of Durham, in 1101. The list goes on to include King David II of Scotland (1346-57), King James I of Scotland (1407-1424), King John of France (1356-60), and his son Philip.

The Tower was not only a prison, among its other uses was as a zoo, which was probably started by a gift of leopards to Henry III from Frederick of Hohenstaufen. In 1255 an elephant arrived as a gift from Louis of France, and then a bear, who was often to be seen fishing with his paws in the river. In 1834, the by then enormous Royal collection of animals became the London Zoo and was moved to Regent's Park.

It has always been an arsenal — in times of war or conflict the armourers have worked long hours honing and cleaning and preparing the weapons. It is a garrison and a fortress — attacked several times but never overrun. It still houses the regimental museum of the Royal Fusiliers (The City of London Regiment). The Astronomer Royal of Charles II, Flamsteed, used the top of the White Tower as his Observatory, until Charles built Flamsteed House for him at Greenwich. The Royal Mint was there as were the Crown Jewels and the Public Records — and of course, above all, it was a Royal Palace. Between the White Tower and the Wakefield Tower stood the Royal apartments and the Great Hall. All of these were pulled down in the time of the Commonwealth so the last king to actually use it as a residence was James I. By tradition the king stayed there the night before he went up river to Westminster for his Coronation.

So much of England's history has taken place inside these walls that it is the most important historical monument in Britain. On a sunny summer's day as you walk around, watching the Beefeaters in their eye-catching uniforms directing the visitors in their amiable way, and you glimpse the river through the trees, it is entrancing. But in the mists of winter the ghosts rise, and one can only too well imagine some of the horrors of the past — and not so distant past as all that, because in the two world wars spies have been executed there by firing squads.

First you must buy your ticket and walk down the Causeway which was the only way into the Tower and which crossed a moat to the Lion Tower, which was where the Royal Menagerie was kept, although the site of it, which is marked in the pavement, does not look large enough to hold the bears and leopards, let alone the elephant!

From the Lion Tower there was a drawbridge to the Middle Tower, then yet another drawbridge to the Byward Tower, where there was a portcullis that can still be seen today and which is still in working order.

The moat was filled in in 1845, so looking at the lovely greensward that has replaced it, it is hard to imagine the deterrent the dark and revolting waters would have been. Quite apart from the Thames water, all the effluent of the Tower went into it, and by all accounts the smell was noxious.

Perhaps the most terrifying way to arrive if you were a state prisoner, and most prisoners in the Tower were (common criminals would have been in Newgate), was by river. That small opening in the outer river wall called Traitor's Gate must have looked like the entrance to Hell to the poor victim. Not every arrival by river was a prisoner about to be incarcerated in the deepest dungeon. It was very common for the king to arrive this way in his State Barge, with the oarsmen clad in Royal livery.

It was here that Elizabeth of York, the eldest daughter of Edward IV arrived to marry Henry VII, a Lancastrian King, and therefore bring to an end the Wars of the Roses, and as a result the Tudor Rose we know today was created — the white rose of York superimposed on the red rose of Lancashire. It was also here that the son of Henry VII, England's most famous (or infamous) king, Henry VIII, waited rapturously for his bride Anne Boleyn, after changing the course of England's history to get her. But sadly she arrived by river again, a bare three years later, to be imprisoned in the Queen's House, where she had stayed before her Coronation, and from there taken to the Great Hall where she was tried and sentenced to be burned or beheaded as pleased the King. For once Henry showed a little kindness and she was allowed death by the sword. The swordsman, an expert, being brought over from Calais for the purpose in 1536.

Henry did not show the same kindness to his fifth Queen, Katherine Howard, who was a cousin of Anne Boleyn. She died by the axe here in 1542. But Anne lived on in history as she was the mother of England's most glorious Queen, Elizabeth I.

Before she became Queen, Elizabeth was sent, as a twenty year old girl, by her half-sister Mary I, who was the daughter of Henry's first wife Catherine of Aragon, to be imprisoned in the Bell Tower. This is the tower you will see on your left as you walk through Byward Tower, and which is attached to the Queen's House. Among the distinguished prisoners who have languished here have been Sir Thomas More, who had been much loved by Henry VIII, but was imprisoned by the King when he refused to swear on the Act of Supremacy. He went to the block on Tower Hill on 7th July 1535. Bishop Fisher of Rochester, died for the same reason in June 1535, having also been incarcerated in the Bell Tower in terrible conditions, and it shows the hardness of Henry's heart when he was thwarted, because Fisher was an old family friend, having been the confessor of Henry's grandmother, Lady Margaret Beaufort. Not quite a year later, the cause of both their troubles, because it was for her that Henry broke with Rome, Anne Boleyn met the same fate.

Another, more handsome inmate of the Bell Tower was James, Duke of Monmouth, who was a natural son of Charles II — his Queen, Catherine of Braganza, was barren. He had no legitimate heirs. After the death of Charles II, in 1684, his brother James II took the Throne, but the Duke of Monmouth led an uprising from the West Country to try and claim the Throne. It was unsuccessful, and no mercy was shown either him or his followers by the Chancellor of James II, Judge Jeffreys — who himself perished in the Bloody Tower in 1689. The Duke of Monmouth was thrown into the Bell Tower and was beheaded forty-eight hours later on Tower Hill, a terrible indignity, because people of the Blood Royal were beheaded on Tower Green, but far worse, was that Jack Ketch the executioner, took five chops to remove his handsome head!

As you walk between the inner and outer walls you come to Traitor's Gate on your right, with St. Thomas's Tower above it, and on your left the Bloody Tower which is built over the gateway into the inner ward. As you will see this has a portcullis as well as very thick doors — all in working order. On the left as you enter you will see a ring on the wall. This was the mooring ring for the boats that came through Traitor's Gate, because originally the steps came right to here.

117

The Bloody Tower received its name after the bloody act of King Richard III in murdering the two young sons of his brother Edward IV. They were Edward V who was awaiting his coronation, and Richard of York. Richard's murderous record must have been hard to beat. It is supposed that he murdered Henry VI by stabbing him in the back while he was at prayer in the Wakefield Tower, then he murdered his own brother, the Duke of Clarence, by drowning him in a butt of malmsey wine in the Bowyer Tower. After a council meeting in the Council Chamber on the top floor of the White Tower, he had Lord Hastings, the great friend of Edward IV, forcibly taken from the chamber, his head put on a convenient log of wood, and summarily despatched. The two little princes, aged 10 and 13, were suffocated when they were asleep, and their bodies thrown under a staircase at the White Tower, where they were not found until the reign of Charles II. He commissioned Sir Christopher Wren to design a casket for their bones which now sits in Westminster Abbey in the appropriately named Innocents Corner.

Sir Walter Raleigh, who was once Captain of the Guard at the Tower, found himself back in the Tower as a prisoner, after plotting to put James I's crown on the head of Arabella Stuart. He was released in 1616 to allow him to make an expedition to the West Indies to look for goldmines. It was an abortive attempt and in 1618 he was back in the Tower where he was kept for six weeks in a dungeon before being beheaded in Old Palace Yard, Westminster. He is buried in the chancel of St. Margaret's, Westminster.

As you emerge from the Bloody Tower you will walk along a high wall towards the next house and then down some steps. This wall was called Raleigh's Walk because this was where he was allowed to take the air.

The half-timbered house next to it, with the guard in his sentry box outside, is the Queen's House, built by Henry VIII. It is now the residence of the Governor and so not accessible to the public. It was in the Council Chamber here that Guy Fawkes and his plotters were examined after being tortured in the cellar of the Wakefield Tower. They were then taken to trial in Westminster Great Hall, and finally hanged, beheaded and quartered in Old Palace Yard.

Another prisoner of Queen's House, Lord Nithsdale, a Scottish lord who supported the Stuarts once the House of Hanover was on the Throne, was much luckier than most. He had a very loving and brave wife who came through snowdrifts from Scotland, bringing with her a maid and two women friends, one of whom she persuaded to wear two dresses. It was the night before he was due to be executed. He donned the extra dress and a hood, held a handkerchief to his face pretending to be weeping — as they all did — and escaped to France!

The most recent prisoner in the Queen's House, is still a prisoner, but not in England — in Spandau — for it was Rudolph Hess, who landed in Scotland in 1941 to sue for peace between Britain and Germany. He was brought to London and treated with dignity in the Tower.

The next house to the Queen's House was the house of the Gentleman Gaoler, where Lady Jane Grey was imprisoned. Hers is a very sad story because she and her husband were the victims of other people's ambitions. She was the grand-daughter of Mary Tudor, who was the sister of Henry VIII. Her claim to the Throne was obviously not as good as Henry's own daughters, Mary and Elizabeth, but after Henry's only son Edward VI died, her pushy father-in-law, the Duke of Northumberland, who had managed to usurp Lord Protector Somerset in his special position with the sickly boy king, and who had succeeded in sending Somerset to the gallows, had her proclaimed Queen. This state only lasted a mere nine days before she found herself a prisoner, and Mary I had rightly claimed her Throne.

For his cruel ambition Northumberland was beheaded on Tower Hill on the 22nd November, 1553, but poor Jane had to wait until the 12th February 1554 for the horror of seeing her husband, Lord Guilford Dudley, who had been imprisoned next to the Gentleman Gaoler's house in the Beauchamp Tower, taken to be beheaded on Tower Hill. And later that same day, as she was looking out of her window, watching the preparations for her own execution on Tower Green, she saw his headless body return in a cart, with his head in a cloth. Beside the window in the main chamber of the Beauchamp Tower, a tower renowned for its inscriptions, is the one pathetic word, carved probably by Lord Guilford Dudley, IANE.

Lord Guilford was not the only one of his family to find

119

himself here in the Tower. All five sons of the Duke of Northumberland were imprisoned here, but not all met the same fate. Robert was condemned to death in 1554, but he was liberated the following year and went on to become the Earl of Leicester, the favourite of Queen Elizabeth I. Ambrose and Henry were both liberated, Ambrose was created the Earl of Warwick in 1561, and Henry was killed at the siege of St. Quentin in 1557, and John Dudley, Earl of Warwick, died in 1554.

Her sister Lady Katherine Grey, was secretly married to Edward Seymour, Earl of Hertford, who was the son of Lord Protector Somerset. She was imprisoned in the Bell Tower by Elizabeth I whose permission they had not sought for the marriage. There she gave birth to a son in 1561. Her husband was imprisoned in the White Tower but they were allowed to meet, and in 1563 a second son was born. The Hertfords were parted for ever, and Lady Katherine was sent to live in Suffolk where she died five years later.

Between the Beauchamp Tower and the White Tower lies the site of the Scaffold, a very sad spot. It was paved in granite by the order of Queen Victoria. It was here that Royalty met its bloody end — in a mercifully more private way than on Tower Hill, which was a large open space north of the Tower where the crowds gathered for the executions. After you leave the Tower cross the road to walk on Tower Hill and look for the commemorative plaques which tell you of these long ago tragedies. Fortunately they are long ago, because the last man to lose his head there was Simon Fraser, Lord Lovat, in 1747. He was one of the Jacobite leaders in the 1745 rebellion and one of the reasons why this execution created such public interest was because Lord Lovat was over 80. As his neck was short he requested to be hanged rather than beheaded but this request was turned down. For his execution many stands were erected for the spectators, but in addition to the excitement of the beheading an unexpected and equally grizzly happening occurred. One of the stands holding the spectators collapsed, killing 20 people and injuring many more. Lord Lovat is said to have died with a benign smile on his face. For every execution a new block was made, and Lord Lovat's block, and the axe that sank 2 inches into it after the stroke, are preserved in the Bowyer

Tower. Lord Lovat's body, along with the bodies of two other Scottish lords, Balmerino and Kilmarnock, lies in St. Peter Ad Vincula, the little church beside Tower Green that was founded in 1185, as do the two queens, Anne Boleyn and Katherine Seymour, Lady Jane Grey and her husband, his father the Duke of Northumberland and his rival the Duke of Somerset, and the poor Duke of Monmouth. Last century the floor of the nave was lifted and all the bodies removed, placed in proper caskets, the soil sieved, and then everything replaced.

After all this gory history a visit to the Jewel Tower, to see the Crown Jewels, would be light relief. Apart from the Ampulla and Anointing Spoon, they were all melted down at the Commonwealth so everything dates from the Restoration, when Charles II commissioned new regalia for his coronation, including a replica of Edward the Confessor's Crown which is the one used for the actual Crowning Ceremony. As this is very heavy it is then replaced by the Crown of State which is also used for the Opening of Parliament.

Some of the jewels are beyond description, among them is a diamond of 530 carats. It is one of the four Stars of Africa and is in the sceptre. Another wonderful jewel is the Black Prince's Balas Ruby which was worn by Henry V at Agincourt and is now in the Imperial State Crown. There is often a queue to see the Crown Jewels but if you possibly can it is worth waiting to see them, as they are unique.

The Jewel House is at one end of Waterloo Barracks, and at the other is the Oriental Gallery. This has a fascinating display of Japanese, Chinese, and Indian armour and weapons, some of which are blood chilling. Probably the most overwhelming exhibit here is the elephant armour, but there are many things that are very interesting.

Behind Waterloo Barracks is the Bowyer Tower which has been designed as an exhibition of torture and imprisonment — it shows you the butt (without the malmsey wine) that the Duke of Clarence was drowned in five hundred years ago.

Next to the Waterloo Barracks, at the end of the Broad Walk, is the Regimental Museum of the Royal Fusiliers. It contains many relics dating from the founding of the Regiment in 1685. Among its trophies and battle honours are three Victoria Crosses. There is also some very fine silver and china.

Last, but very much not least, a visit to the oldest and most historic building in this fascinating complex of buildings — the White Tower. Work on this 90ft. tall tower began in 1078, and from 1100, with Ranulph Flambard as its first inmate, it received its fair share of prisoners. Ranulph was one of the lucky ones who got away. Some friends brought him a jug of wine, in which they concealed a rope. Flambard used the wine to make his guards drowsy and then sensibly climbed out of the window and escaped to Normandy. The last native Prince of Wales, Griffith, was not so lucky. He was imprisoned in the Tower in 1244 and he followed Flambard's example. He made a rope of sheets and hangings which he attached to the top of the Tower (there must have been many sheets to drop 90ft.). But as he climbed down his line gave way and he plunged to his death with his head being crushed to his shoulders. His son Llewellyn, who had also been a prisoner in the Tower, managed to escape, but was recaptured near Builth in Wales. There was a prophesy that he would wear his crown in London so Edward I had his head chopped off and set atop the White Tower with a crown of ivy leaves! At the expulsion of the Jews from England in 1278 Edward I herded 600 into one of the dungeons, the conditions were terrible and over 200 died. After the Siege of Calais by Edward III the Commander and twelve Burghers were brought to the Tower.

The White Tower was not only a prison. It houses the oldest church in London, the Chapel of St. John. In this chapel Henry VI lay in state after his murder by Richard III. Elizabeth of York, the consort of Henry VII, who died in childbirth on her thirty-eighth birthday, lay in state with 800 candles round her, and Mary I married by proxy, Philip of Spain.

The White Tower contains the national collection of weapons and armour, some of them of very great interest like the suit of armour which is 6ft. 10ins. high. Just the sight of this giant coming towards them must have made the enemy flee. The armour of Henry VIII gives a fascinating view of the man who was a tyrant, but who was also very popular. From his armour when he was young and handsome, to the armour when he was middle-aged and gross.

From this floor you will descend by 114 steps to the dungeons which now house the cannon and mortar. You will also see the well which was sunk in the 12th century and which is 40ft. deep.

After leaving the White Tower walk down the slope towards the river taking care to avoid those nasty black birds — the Ravens. There are six. They have their own quarters, their own ration allowance, and they may go anywhere they like in the Tower, but they can't leave the Tower because their wings are clipped. Legend has it that if they do leave the Tower it will fall.

One of the important rituals of the Tower is the Ceremony of the Keys. This is performed each night at 10 p.m. and is the ceremonial locking of the main gate.

Go through the outer wall on to the Wharf which was originally constructed in 1228 with earth taken from the moat when it was dug. There are a number of interesting guns along this pleasant walk and they always seem to have small boys sitting on them. On Royal occasions the Honourable Artillery Company fires Royal salutes, 62 guns on the anniversary of the birth, accession, or coronation of the Sovereign, and 41 guns on the birth of a Prince or a Princess, and other Royal occasions.

For lunch, you can either eat where the lions and leopards once, did, in the restaurant which is on the site of the Lion Tower, or you can turn left, walk under Tower Bridge and along the edge of the river into St. Katherine's Dock. Cross over the lock and go to the Dickens Inn. This was once a rope store, but has recently, and very successfully, been turned into a pub. They serve salad lunches on the ground floor bar, and on the two floors above they have more conventional, more expensive restaurants. All good.

After lunch have a stroll round the dock because it is a very interesting example of what can be done to a decaying district. It is now a very attractive leisure area, with classy yachts instead of the cargo ships which once lay there. What used to be the ivory warehouse had now been converted into delightful apartments, and there are shops, pubs, several good restaurants and a hotel with a lovely view over the river.

The inner dock has been converted into a maritime museum, with many interesting vessels to see, but the museum ship to now venture on is the H.M.S. Belfast, which lies in the Thames upstream from the Tower, so retrace your steps to the entrance to the Tower where you find a kiosk to pay.

The Belfast is a Southampton class cruiser of 11,500 tons, built in 1937. She took part in the Battle of North Cape, took a leading part in Normandy, and was in Korea. When she was about to be pensioned off she was bought by a trust who have opened her to the public. You can tour the ship, going up and down ladders, sitting in gun turrets and in the wireless operator's room, imagining how it really was, although the Thames can never be a substitute for the rough sea of the North Cape.

And now back to dry land. After a day immersed in Britain's history from the Romans to Korea, from wicked uncles to martyred queens, you probably feel like putting your feet up and having a good cup of tea — or perhaps something even stronger.

Although these ten days will give you plenty of facts, and a great deal of history, I hope you never hesitate, as you wander around, to digress and investigate anything you spot that interests you. When there's something you'd rather do — like exploring London's newest cultural centre at the Barbican or the shops and restaurants on the historic site of Covent Garden vegetable market — then do it. I want you to enjoy London as much as I do.

POPULAR MEDICAL AND TRAVEL TITLES
From SETTLE & BENDALL (WIGMORE)

HOW TO SURVIVE YOUR HOLIDAY £8.95 hard 0 907070 04 3 ☐
The Traveller's Guide to Health
by Dr C. Allan Birch £3.95 paper 0 909070 05 1 ☐

The first holiday/travel book to be written by a qualified medical practitioner giving much needed reliable information on how to avoid accidents and sudden ailments.

THE HERPES MANUAL £7.99 hard 0 907070 17 5 ☐
The Book for everyone concerned
about Herpes
by Sue Blanks and Carole Woddis £2.99 paper 0 907070 18 3 ☐

Genital Herpes is on the increase and continually in the news. This new manual — written by sufferers for all members of the public — offers a practical guide to overcoming the physical and emotional effects of this incurable sexually transmitted disease.

FRANCE FOR EVERYONE £7.95 hard 0 907070 15 9 ☐
A Guide to Easy Travelling
by Inge and James Moore £2.95 paper 0 907070 16 7 ☐

Package holidays are a rarity in France. This book answers all the basic questions to provide you with a carefree holiday and best value from France. A guide itself and a guide to the guides.

THE MIRACLE OF YOU £2.75 paper 0 950743305 ☐
How to relieve many common ailments
by the application of Zone Therapy
by Joseph Corvo

Mr Corvo offers a straightforward illustrated account of his techniques.

Buy them at your local bookshops or send in this coupon to

- -

SETTLE & BENDALL (Reader Service Dept.)
32 Savile Row, London W1X 1AG

Please send me the book(s) I have ticked. I am enclosing £
(please add 30p to cover postage and handling in UK).

Mr/Mrs/Miss ....

Address ....

....

....

POPULAR TITLES
From SETTLE & BENDALL (Wigmore)

SUPERSECRETARY   £5.95 hard 0 907070 00 0 ☐
Your Office Survival Guide
by Sally Denholm-Young   £2.95 paper 0 907070 01 9 ☐

Nationally reviewed. Heralded as 'All you ever need to know' by popular magazines and described as 'an interesting and enlightening book' by Society of Commercial Teachers.

SO YOU WANT TO BE AN ANGEL? £6.95 hard 0 907070 02 7 ☐
The Nurses' Survival Guide
by K. Barry Napier   £3.95 paper 0 907070 03 5 ☐

An accurate, entertaining and by definition controversial account of the real conditions and working environment of nurses.

TOO LATE TO TURN BACK   £7.95 hard 0 907070 06 X ☐
Barbara and Graham Greene in Liberia
by Barbara Greene

No one who knows Graham Greene's Journey Without Maps should fail to read this quite different account of the dangerous, thrilling expedition . . .

Buy them at your local bookshops or send in this coupon to

SETTLE & BENDALL (Reader Service Dept.)
32 Savile Row, London W1X 1AG

Please send me the book(s) I have ticked. I am enclosing £
(please add 30p to cover postage and handling in UK).

Mr/Mrs/Miss . . . .

Address . . . .

. . . .

. . . .